Praise for Other Books by Kaye Thomas

"Extremely thorough, but easily understood." *Joseph Hurley, author, The Best Way to Save for College*

"Belongs in every serious investor's library." *Peter Hupalo, author, Becoming An Investor: Building Wealth by Investing in Stocks, Bonds, and Mutual Funds*

"A must-read." *Bruce Brumberg, Editor-in-Chief, myStockOptions.com*

"Written in a way that's useful to experts and understandable to those who are not."—*Corey Rosen, Executive Director, National Center for Employee Ownership*

"Does a great job of explaining the rules."—*Gordon Rapkin, Executive Vice President, Chief Marketing Officer, Transcentive*

"A comprehensive information resource."—*Debra Sherman, Foundation for Enterprise Development*

"Should be required reading for anybody receiving options as compensation."—*Roy Lewis, co-author, The Motley Fool's Investment Tax Guide*

Praise for Our Web Site (fairmark.com)

"One of our favorite sites."—*Newsweek Magazine,*

"One of the top 50 financial web sites."—*Money Magazine*

"A good newsy site, easy to navigate and fun to read. Its explanations are crystal clear."—*The Boston Globe*

Also by the Author

Consider Your Options: Get the Most from Your Equity Compensation

Capital Gains, Minimal Taxes: The Essential Guide for Investors and Traders

Fairmark Guide
to the
Roth IRA

Retirement Planning in Plain Language

2004 Edition

Kaye A. Thomas

A Plain Language Guide From
FAIRMARK PRESS INC. LISLE, ILLINOIS

Fairmark Guide to the Roth IRA

Retirement Planning in Plain Language

This printing of *Fairmark Guide to the Roth IRA* reflects relevant legal authorities as of January 6, 2004.

Published by:

Fairmark Press Inc.
P.O. Box 353
Lisle, Illinois 60532

www.fairmark.com
(630)728-3835

First printing of 2004 edition, January 2004
Printed in the United States of America

Publisher's Cataloging-in-Publication Data
Thomas, Kaye A.
Fairmark guide to the Roth IRA : retirement planning in plain language / Kaye A. Thomas. — 2004 ed.
p. cm.
Includes bibliographical references and index.
LCCN: 2003099712
ISBN: 0-9674981-0-4

1. Individual retirement accounts—United States. I. Title.

HG1660.U5T46 2004 332.024'0145
QBI03-200965

Table of Contents

About the Author

Kaye Thomas has over 20 years of experience as a tax lawyer dealing with tax matters relating to business transactions, finance and compensation. He now spends most of his time as a writer and publisher of books and other materials relating to taxation and investments.

Kaye also maintains a free web site called the *Tax Guide for Investors* at **www.fairmark.com**, providing hundreds of pages of plain language tax guidance. The web site also features a message board where Kaye and other tax professionals respond to questions and comments from readers.

Kaye's law degree is from Harvard Law School, where he served as an editor of the *Harvard Law Review* and graduated *cum laude* in 1980.

Dedication

Part of this dedication must go to William V. Roth, Jr., for whom the Roth IRA is named. I was saddened to learn of his death shortly before this book went to press.

The Roth IRA's success is partly built on the efforts of many people to help tax practitioners and the general public understand how it works. The honor roll includes Treasury staff who worked hard to issue helpful regulations as promptly as possible; Gregory Kolojeski, editor of the *Roth IRA Website* at www.rothira.com and co-author of *Roth IRA Answer Book*; and the many experts who have responded to thousands of questions (over 4,000 of them about the Roth IRA!) on the message board of our web site at www.fairmark.com. I salute them all.

Part I
What Hath Roth Wrought

This part of the book provides an introduction to the Roth IRA and a first take on whether the Roth IRA is the right choice for you.

Part I: What Hath Roth Wrought

Chapter 1
Introducing the Roth IRA

The Roth IRA was born on January 1, 1998 as a result of the Taxpayer Relief Act of 1997.

For many people—for most, in fact—the Roth IRA is an excellent way to build retirement wealth. It provides no deduction for contributions, but instead offers a benefit that isn't available for any other form of retirement savings: if you meet certain requirements, all earnings are tax free when you or your beneficiary withdraw them. Other benefits include avoiding the early distribution penalty on certain withdrawals, and avoiding the need to take minimum distributions after age 70½.

Plus and Minus

The chief advantage of the Roth IRA is obvious: the ability to have investment earnings completely escape taxation. The advantage comes at a price, though: you don't get a deduction when you contribute to the Roth IRA.

So which is more important? It depends on your personal situation, and also on what assumptions you want to make about the future. How long before you withdraw money from your IRA? What will your tax bracket be then? What investment earnings can you anticipate in the interim?

You can do lots of fancy analysis, but the bottom line is that most people are better off in the Roth IRA. The chief reason is that the Roth IRA is effectively bigger than a traditional IRA because it holds after-tax dollars. If you can take advantage of this feature of the Roth IRA by maximizing your contributions you'll add greater tax leverage to your retirement savings.

There are two other significant advantages to the Roth IRA. One is that the minimum distribution rules don't apply. If you're able to live on other resources after retirement, you don't have to draw on your Roth IRA at age 70½. That means your earnings continue to grow tax-free. The other advantage is the ability to take certain early distributions without paying the early distribution penalty. In short, the Roth IRA makes it easier to keep your money in, and also easier to take your money out.

Eligibility

You can establish a Roth IRA if you're eligible for a regular contribution to a Roth IRA or a rollover (or conversion) to a Roth IRA.

You're eligible to make a regular contribution to a Roth IRA even if you participate in a retirement plan maintained by your employer. These contributions can be as much as $3,000 ($3,500 if you're 50 or older by the end of the year).* There are just two requirements. First, you or your spouse must have compensation or alimony income equal to the amount contributed. And second, your modified adjusted gross income can't exceed certain limits. For the maximum contribution, the limits are $95,000 for single individuals and $150,000 for married individuals filing joint returns. The amount you can contribute is reduced gradually and then completely eliminated when your modified adjusted gross income

* These limits are in effect for 2003 and 2004.

exceeds $110,000 (single) or $160,000 (married filing jointly).

You can convert your traditional IRA to a Roth IRA (or a rollover from a traditional IRA to a Roth IRA) if (a) your modified adjusted gross income is $100,000 or less, and (b) you're single or file jointly with your spouse. You'll have to pay tax in the year of the conversion, but for many people the long-term savings outweigh the conversion tax.

Distributions

Distributions from Roth IRAs are tax-free until you've withdrawn all your regular contributions. After that you'll withdraw your rollover (conversion) contributions, if any. Special rules apply when you withdraw your conversion contributions. When you've withdrawn all your contributions (regular and rollover), any subsequent withdrawals come from earnings. The withdrawals are tax-free if you're over age 59½ and at least five years have expired since you established your Roth IRA. Otherwise (with limited exceptions) they're taxable and potentially subject to the early distribution penalty.

Chapter 2
Is a Roth Right for You?

Rules of thumb in choosing where to save.

There's an entire section of this book dealing with Roth IRA decision factors. This chapter offers a preview in the form of relatively brief rules of thumb about when it makes sense to choose the Roth IRA. For the reasoning behind these conclusions, read the relevant chapters in the section dealing with decision factors.

Roth IRA vs. Taxable Account

One of the alternatives to a Roth IRA is a regular taxable account with a bank, mutual fund or stockbroker. Either way you get no deduction when money goes in. The Roth IRA provides earnings that are tax-deferred and possibly tax-free. But if you make a taxable withdrawal of earnings from the Roth IRA, you'll report ordinary income (not long-term capital gain), and you may pay a 10% early distribution penalty.

- Choose the Roth IRA over a taxable account if you expect to leave the earnings in the IRA long enough to qualify for tax-free distributions. Remember, you can withdraw *contributions* tax-free at any time, but *earnings* generally have to stay in until you're 59½ and have satisfied the five-year requirement.

- If you expect to withdraw earnings when they're taxable, you're generally better off with a taxable account—especially if you're investing for long-term capital gains, or if the 10% early distribution penalty will apply.

Roth IRA vs. Nondeductible IRA

If you participate in a retirement plan maintained by your employer and your income is above certain levels, you may face a choice between saving in a Roth IRA or making a nondeductible contribution to a traditional IRA. In either case you get no deduction for your contribution, but the Roth IRA provides greater flexibility in withdrawing your contributions, and the possibility of withdrawing your earnings tax-free.

- Choose the Roth IRA over a nondeductible contribution to a traditional IRA in all cases.

Roth IRA vs. Deductible IRA

The choice between saving in a Roth IRA and making a deductible contribution to a traditional IRA is more difficult. The traditional IRA gives you a deduction when you contribute, but the Roth IRA gives you a chance to have earnings that are entirely tax-free for decades to come. Here are the main ideas:

- If you're saving the maximum amount each year, the Roth IRA is likely to be better.
- If you're in a low tax bracket when saving, the Roth IRA is likely to be better.
- Conversely, if you're in a high tax bracket when you contribute and expect to be in a much lower tax bracket when you withdraw your earnings, a traditional IRA may be the better choice.

Roth IRA vs. Employer Plan

If your employer provides a 401k or similar plan, you may face a choice between contributing to that plan or a Roth IRA. Don't forget you can do both!

- Choose your employer's 401k or similar plan if your employer will make matching contributions, and you don't expect to forfeit the matching contributions by quitting before they're vested.
- Otherwise choose as you would when deciding between a Roth IRA and a deductible IRA (see above).

Rules of Thumb for Conversions

Finally we come to the most complicated choice: whether to convert (roll over) your traditional IRA to a Roth IRA.

- Generally you shouldn't roll to a Roth IRA if you need to hold out some of the IRA money to pay taxes on the conversion and you'll pay the 10% early distribution penalty on the amount you hold out.
- If your retirement tax bracket will be 15%, avoid paying 25% or higher on your rollover. Remember that a partial rollover may permit you to avoid pushing into a higher tax bracket in the year of the rollover.
- If your traditional IRA contains mostly nondeductible contributions, rolling it to a Roth IRA should produce handsome benefits.
- Even if all contributions to your traditional IRA were deductible, rolling it to a Roth IRA may produce benefits if the first two points above don't apply.

- Once again, these are merely rules of thumb. In most cases they give the right results, but your particular situation may call for a different answer. An extended discussion of all the factors that go into choosing a Roth IRA appears in Part VII.

Part II
Getting Started

In this part we learn some basics about IRAs in general, then walk step by step through the process of setting up a Roth IRA. If you need guidance on how to invest your savings, the last chapter in this section provides a short course in investing.

Part II: Getting Started

Chapter 3
First, Some General Rules

A few things you should know before starting an IRA.

Most of the rules that apply to traditional IRAs also apply to Roth IRAs. There are important differences, of course, and those are spelled out in other chapters. This chapter summarizes some of the most important rules that apply to both types of IRAs.

Trust or Custodial Account

Your IRA must be maintained as a trust or custodial account at a bank, a federally insured credit union, a savings and loan association, or an entity approved by the IRS to act as trustee or custodian. Other approved entities include mutual funds, stock brokers and insurance companies. The assets of your IRA can't be commingled with other assets (for example, you can't have a joint IRA with your spouse).

Contributions

There are special rules for Roth IRA contributions. But some rules for traditional IRA contributions apply to the Roth IRA, too.

Timing

You can set up a Roth IRA at any time. However, you can make contributions for a given year only during the period that begins on the first day of the year and ends on the due date of your return for the year—not including extensions. If you file your tax returns on the calendar year (as nearly all people do), you can make your contribution for any year during the period from January 1 of that year until April 15 of the following year. (If April 15 falls on a weekend or holiday, the deadline is the first weekday after April 15 that isn't a holiday.)

If you make a contribution to an IRA on or before April 15 it's important to designate whether the contribution is for the current year or the preceding one.

- When you designate a contribution for the previous year, you're treated as if you made the contribution on December 31.

You can file your tax return before you make your contribution. If you do this, report the contribution that you intend to make (if you're contributing to a traditional IRA). If you end up not making the contribution, you should file an amended return notifying the IRS of this fact. (Contributions to Roth IRAs aren't deductible, so you don't have to report these contributions on your return in any event.)

Cash Only

Your regular (non-rollover) contribution to an IRA must be made in cash (including checks and money orders, of course). You're not allowed to contribute property (such as stocks and bonds) except when you're completing a rollover from another IRA.

Prohibited Transactions

There are various things you're not permitted to do with a traditional IRA. The same rules apply to Roth IRAs. Examples of prohibited transactions:

- Borrowing from your IRA or using it as security for a loan.
- Selling property to your IRA, or buying property from it.
- Buying property for your personal use with funds held by your IRA (before the funds have been distributed to you).
- Investing your IRA in certain "collectibles," such as artwork, stamps or coins.

Chapter 4
How to Start a Roth IRA

Practical guidance on how to set up a Roth IRA.

Starting a Roth IRA is easy. Any number of providers are more than happy to make this process easy for you. This chapter covers both the thought process you should go through and the practical steps you need to take.

Outline

To start a Roth IRA you need to take the following steps:

- Confirm that you're eligible for a Roth IRA.
- Determine that a Roth IRA is your best choice.
- Decide what type of investment is most appropriate for your Roth IRA.
- Select a provider for your Roth IRA.
- Establish the IRA.

Eligibility

It's your responsibility—not the IRA provider's—to determine that you're eligible to establish a Roth IRA. And there's no point in setting one up if you'll merely have to undo the process later. Most people with earned income above $3,000 and "modified adjusted gross income" below $95,000 ($150,000 for married couples filing jointly) are eligible to contribute $3,000 to a Roth IRA. See the chapters dealing with regular contributions and conversions to confirm that you're eligible.

Choosing the Roth IRA

Naturally, before you set up a Roth IRA you want to determine whether a Roth IRA is the right choice for your retirement savings. Chapter 2 gave a quick overview of this issue, and you'll find much more discussion of the pros and cons throughout this book.

Type of Investment

People sometimes ask what kind of investment return they can expect from a Roth IRA. The answer depends on the type of investment you choose. The best type of investment for your Roth IRA depends on various factors:

- The size of your Roth IRA
- The time frame for your investment
- Your other investments
- Your investing style

Size of Your Roth IRA

The tax law doesn't set a minimum size for a Roth IRA, but providers generally set minimum account sizes. If one provider won't accept your account because it's too small, try another. In any event, if you're starting small, it makes sense to choose a simple investment that won't incur a lot of fees or require a lot of attention. You can get fancy after you've built your IRA to a larger size.

Time Frame

When investing for the long term it makes sense to take some risk to obtain higher rewards. If the risk produces losses, you'll have plenty of time to recover. Short term investors need to put more emphasis on asset protection.

Your Other Investments

If you have other savings, such as a brokerage account or a 401k account, consider whether your IRA can be invested in a way that provides more balance to your overall portfolio. Another consideration is the allocation of assets between taxable accounts and non-taxable accounts. For example, some advisors suggest keeping assets that produce mostly ordinary income (like interest or dividends that don't qualify for the 15% rate) in an IRA or other non-taxable account, and investing your taxable accounts in assets that produce long-term capital gain or qualifying dividends.

Your Investing Style

Choose an investment you're comfortable with. Some investors are willing to risk losses in order to have a shot at higher gains. Others are willing to accept a lower return to get a greater feeling of security.

Investing style affects your choice in another way. Some types of investments do quite well if you ignore them for extended periods. Others need frequent attention. How much time and effort do you want to put into your IRA investments?

Select a Provider

It's easy enough to find an IRA provider. But which one is best for you?

can set up a Roth IRA with a financial institution and contribute up to $3,000. Instead, if your company offers this option, you can establish a deemed IRA within the company's retirement plan. You can make the same Roth IRA contribution there, even though you already made the maximum 401k contribution.

When you want to take the money out, you're subject to all the same rules as if this were a separate Roth IRA. This account is not governed by the rules that apply to 401k accounts.

Example: Your company's 401k plan allows you to borrow from your account. You aren't allowed to borrow from an IRA, so you won't be allowed to borrow from the deemed IRA, even though it's part of an employer plan.

Advantages

A deemed Roth IRA does not have special tax advantages over a Roth IRA you set up with a financial institution. Instead, it may provide some *practical* advantages.

For one thing, you may arrange for the company to make contributions directly from your salary. That won't change the way you're taxed on your salary, but it can be convenient and help you stick to the discipline of saving regularly.

There's further convenience in not having to figure out where to establish your IRA and evaluate the wide world of investment choices. Your employer has already done the work of determining that the investment opportunities in the retirement plan are sound.

If your company's plan offers attractive investment alternatives, this could be another boost for the idea of a deemed IRA. Large retirement plans often get a better deal on their investments than individual investors (for example, lower management fees), and you can benefit indirectly by establishing your Roth IRA within the company's plan.

Disadvantages

You should get all the same tax advantages (and disadvantages) from a deemed Roth IRA as you would from a Roth IRA you set up with a financial institution. Here again we have to focus on practical issues to find disadvantages.

Employers usually put some work into making good investment alternatives available in their retirement plan, but they don't all do a good job in this area. If your company's plan offers lousy investments, the deemed IRA doesn't make a lot of sense. Likewise, you should avoid this choice if you'll be under pressure to invest in your company's stock, if you prefer to diversify.

Consider also whether your company does a good job handling the administrative details of its retirement plan. Do they provide clear, accurate financial statements in a timely manner? When you have questions, can you get answers? If you're unhappy with the way they run the 401k, there's a good chance you'll be unhappy with the way they run your deemed IRA.

Chapter 6
A Short Course in Investing

What every IRA owner should know about investing.

There are thousands of books about investing. Many of them are longer than this book, so obviously I can't distill their essence into a single chapter. What's more, even the experts can't agree on what makes a good investment. This chapter briefly summarizes the principles I personally rely on in making investment decisions. I'm not an investment advisor and I don't have expert credentials in this area, but I've read dozens of books on the subject and believe the following information is sound. If you're new to investing, or simply haven't found time to make a study of the subject, the following may keep you from going too far wrong.

Three Pillars

A sound investment strategy is built on three pillars. If any one of them is missing, there's a good chance you'll look back later with regret.

- **Risk.** You have to take some risk with your investments if you want your money to grow. Yet too much risk is, well, too much. When I hear about someone who turned a large IRA into a small one (or a 401k into a "201k") it's always someone who took too much risk.

- **Return.** If you focus too much on risk, you'll make investments that don't grow fast enough—in other words, investments that don't provide enough investment *return*. To be a successful investor you need a balance between risk and return.

- **Expenses.** Expenses can turn a good return into a lousy one. One of your biggest challenges as an investor is to be aware of expenses, including hidden ones.

Risk

There's no magic formula for the amount of risk you should take. Risk is related to reward, so a lot depends on your age, financial goals and earning capacity. Your appetite for risk matters, too. If losses will make your stomach churn, steer for calmer waters, even if that means the growth prospects for your savings are more modest.

Asset Allocation

One way to manage risk is to divide your investments among different kinds of assets. This is called *asset allocation*. You decide how much money to put in each of the three main categories:

- *Stocks*. Stocks provide investment returns in the form of dividends and capital gains. Historically, stocks have provided the highest returns, but also the highest risk.

- *Bonds*. Bonds provide investment returns in the form of interest, and can also produce capital gains. They expose you to less risk than stocks, but you can still lose money, even if the bond is guaranteed.

- *Cash.* The safest investments are provided by money market funds and similar vehicles. Investment pros refer to these investments as *cash* even though they're actually short-term debt obligations.

Long-term investors should normally have most of their money in stocks. This is where you're likely to get the highest returns, and with a long time horizon you can recover from losses that may occur in any particular downturn. It's a good idea to have some money in bonds as well, and increase the proportion in bonds as you move closer to the time when you'll use the money. Cash is a good choice for your emergency stash or for any money you expect to use in the near future, but not a good choice for long-term investments. Money market returns are so paltry they sometimes grow slower than the rate of inflation, which means this "safe" investment can actually shrink with time.

Real estate? Some advisors push the idea of using your IRA to invest in real estate. There's a good way to do this and a bad way.

- *Good.* Invest part of your IRA in a real estate investment trust (REIT), or in a mutual fund that invests in REITs. When you invest in a REIT, you get professional management and diversification. Like other investments, REITs perform well during some periods and poorly during others. Think of them as something like bonds, an investment that can reduce risk in a portfolio that is otherwise mainly made up of business stocks.

- *Bad.* At some point you're likely to encounter an advisor, book or web site that recommends direct ownership of real estate in your IRA. My strong conviction is that this is a truly lousy idea. The tax law is loaded with provisions that provide advantages for real estate investments *outside* an IRA, and *dis*advantages for real estate investments *inside* an IRA. When you put real estate in an IRA (other than through a REIT), you're going out of your way to make your life difficult.

Diversification

The second big way to manage risk is *diversification.* I should have a separate chapter on this topic because this is where many people go wrong. Yet telling investors about diversification is a lot like telling teenagers to keep their room neat and take out the trash. Some of them get it, but a lot don't. So I'm just going to state the simple facts as I see them and let you decide what to do.

There are thousands of books, web sites, newsletters and magazine articles that purport to explain how to choose stocks or mutual funds that will do better than the overall stock market. Many of them are interesting and some sound quite convincing, but they are all unreliable. No one knows with any degree of certainty which stocks or mutual funds will do well over the next month, or the next year, or the next ten years. Even the best stock pickers make plenty of mistakes. What's more, stocks and mutual funds with terrific performance in the recent past often follow up with performance that is downright terrible.

The best way to deal with this uncertainty is to invest in a large number of different stocks in a large number of different segments of the economy. Don't load up on the stock of the company where you work. Don't load up on stocks in your own company's industry. Don't restrict yourself to interesting stocks. Buy lots of stocks in different industries, or invest in one or more mutual funds that buy lots of stocks in different industries.

Do you love tech stocks? Many people do. A few years ago, many people loved them to death. Guess what happened to their IRAs?

> ▪ The single biggest investment mistake you can make with your IRA is to fail to diversify. Over the long haul, investors who diversify get returns at least as good as those who do not, at substantially lower risk.

Return

The second pillar is investment return. I've already given you the main facts of life here:

- Money market funds and other cash investments provide paltry returns and should be used mainly for money that must be kept safe, such as the amount you've set aside to pay your taxes in April.
- Bonds provide decent returns at lower risk than stocks, although you should be aware that you can lose money on bonds. If interest rates change, a bond can lose value even if it's guaranteed by (or issued by) the United States government.
- Stocks expose you to greater risk but historically have provided greater returns than other investments.

The advantage of stocks over other investments is large enough so that I feel nearly everyone who is investing for the long term should have a significant part of his or her portfolio in stocks, or in mutual funds that invest in stocks. A bear market (declining stock prices) can be a painful experience, but stocks have always pulled ahead in the past and it seems likely this will be true in the future.

Expenses

This is another major area where investors go wrong. It's not the most fascinating topic in the world, but investors who pay attention to this area tend to come out ahead—in the long run, *way* ahead.

Some expenses are easy to spot. If your IRA provider charges an annual fee, that will be disclosed and you'll see it on your statement. If you set up your IRA in a brokerage account and buy and sell stocks, you'll see the account reduced by brokerage commissions.* Other expenses are hidden, and hidden expenses can eat you alive.

Costs of trading. Buying and selling stocks can be a lot more expensive than you may think. Brokerage commissions, the *visible* cost of trading, are just the start of the story. The amount you lose on the so-called bid-ask spread can be more significant. This is the difference between what sellers are asking and buyers are bidding for the stock you're trading. You pay the higher price when you buy and get the lower price when you sell. You can also lose money on poor execution by your broker (failing to get the best available price). It might seem that people who trade stocks frequently have an advantage because they can adjust their investments to the latest news. The reality is that frequent traders usually lose money rapidly because the expenses of trading overwhelm any advantage.

Mutual fund loads. Some mutual funds charge a sales fee, called a *load,* when you buy shares. You may pay

* IRA owners sometimes ask if they can use "outside" money to pay these commissions so the value of the IRA is preserved. The answer is *no.* If you pay these commissions with money from outside the IRA, you're treated as having made a contribution to the IRA, which is subject to all the usual rules for contributions. A regular annual fee is different: you can pay that with "outside" money.

when your money goes in, or when your money comes out, or pay something every year. The sales fee may go to a financial advisor who recommended the fund.

There's nothing wrong with paying a load if you get something of reasonable value in return. Some financial advisors get a significant part of their compensation this way, and provide valuable advice and other services in return. You need to be aware of how much you're paying, though, and compare it with what you're receiving. If you put $40,000 into a mutual fund that charges a 5% load up front, your account will start with only $38,000, and the account will have to earn $2,000 just to get you back to where you were before you invested.

There are plenty of *no-load* mutual funds that charge no sales fees. Some experts believe these mutual funds perform just as well as the ones that charge fees, and suggest you should always stick with no-load funds. That's fine too, but then if you seek professional investment advice you'll have to pay for it some other way.

Other mutual fund expenses. Unfortunately there's more to the story. Mutual funds differ greatly in the amount of expenses they incur each year. Some of the expenses are disclosed and some are not. Even if you focus only on the part that is disclosed, you can come out ahead by favoring mutual funds that have a low expense ratio. There's a lot of evidence that these funds, as a group, outperform funds where the expenses are high.

A Simple Plan

If you're new to investing and all this seems like a lot to absorb, here's a simple plan. I don't say it's the best idea for everyone, but it's a way to do reasonably well until you get comfortable with an investment advisor or with your own knowledge of the subject.

Step one: asset allocation. Decide how much money to put in stocks. If you're investing for a long time—15 years or more—make sure you have a significant chunk of your money here because this is where it is likely to do the best. Dial back on your stock allocation if you're retired, or close to retirement, or otherwise expect to need the money soon. Dial it back also if the thought of losing money in a bear market makes you sick. Divide the rest between bonds and cash, bearing in mind that bonds involve more risk than cash but provide higher returns in the long run.

- Can't decide how much goes where? The formula used by many people is 60% stocks and 40% bonds. There's nothing magical about that formula, and nothing wrong with choosing a higher or lower stock allocation. Yet you'll have plenty of company if you use that allocation.

Step two: choose mutual funds. For most investors, the best way to invest is through mutual funds. You can get professional management and instant diversification at a modest cost. If you're just starting to invest, this is the way to go.

But which mutual funds? Choose one or more no-load funds from major companies. Make sure they cover all segments of the economy, not just tech stocks or whatever else is the flavor of the month. And make sure the expense ratio is low.

The easy way to get a broad-based mutual fund that has a low expense ratio is to look for an *index fund.* This is a mutual fund that tries to imitate the performance of a stock market index, such as the S&P 500 index. Beware of narrow indexes, though. The Nasdaq index, for example, is heavy in tech stocks and can lose a lot of value in a short period of time.

Last Words

I want to stress again that this is not the only way to invest, or necessarily the best. There's no reason to distrust an advisor who recommends a different approach. This is simply a starting point for people who need one—and it also happens to be the way I've invested my own IRA.

Reading list. If you want to learn more about this subject, here are a few of my favorite books. First, on the subject of accumulating wealth, try *The Richest Man in Babylon* by George S. Clason. This thought-provoking little book deserves its status as a perennial best-seller. Another excellent book in this category is Stanley & Danko's *Millionaire Next Door.*

On the subject of investing in general, anything by Andrew Tobias is good, especially *The Only Investment Guide You'll Ever Need.* Jane Bryant Quinn provides excellent coverage of all kinds of personal finance issues, including investing. So does Suze Orman—her status as a television performer is built on solid knowledge and good judgment.

For stocks in particular, Peter Lynch's books are interesting and witty, but for a solid understanding of the subject, two books are indispensable: *A Random Walk Down Wall Street* by Burton G. Malkiel, and *Stocks for the Long Run* by Jeremy J. Siegel. On the subject of mutual funds, anything by John Bogle is worth reading.

Part III
Annual Contributions

This section of the book explains the rules for making annual contributions—in other words, contributions other than rollover or conversion contributions. Most people can contribute $3,000 per year to a Roth IRA (reduced by any amount they contribute to a traditional IRA), but there are restrictions. You or your spouse must have compensation or alimony income, and your overall income can't exceed certain limits.

Part III: Annual Contributions

Chapter 7
Basic Rules for Annual Contributions

Main rules for annual contributions to a Roth IRA.

Most people who work for a living (or have a spouse who works for a living) can contribute $3,000 per year to a Roth IRA. Those who can't contribute $3,000 fall into two categories: those who don't have enough compensation or alimony income, and those who have too much overall income.

First, the Good News

Before we turn to the actual limit, here are some items that don't affect your contributions.

No Age Limit

There's no age limit for contributions to Roth IRAs. For traditional IRAs, you lose the ability to make contributions in the year you turn age 70½. Not so for Roth IRAs. If you meet the other requirements, you can set up a brand new Roth IRA at age 85 and begin saving for your "retirement"!

There's also no lower age limit. A minor can set up a Roth IRA and contribute to it. (See Chapter XX.) But remember, young or old, you need to have compensation income, as explained later.

No Employer Plan Limit

Coverage under a retirement plan maintained by your employer does not affect your ability to contribute to a Roth IRA. If you meet the requirements described below, you can contribute to a Roth IRA even if you're covered by an employer plan or 401k.

Conversion Doesn't Affect Annual Contribution

The limit on regular contributions to a Roth IRA is entirely independent of whether you made a rollover or conversion. You can make a regular (non-rollover) contribution even if you've made a conversion during the same year.

Contribution to Conversion Roth IRA

Although there was initially some confusion on this point, it's now clear that you can make regular contributions to a conversion Roth IRA.

The Contribution Limit

The basic limit for annual contributions to a Roth IRA (other than rollover contributions) is $3,000 ($3,500 if you're age 50 or older by the end of the year).* But this limit may be reduced for any of the following reasons:

- You or your spouse may not have enough compensation or alimony income to contribute the full amount.
- Your contribution may be reduced or eliminated because your modified adjusted gross income is too large.
- Your limitation is reduced if you've made certain other contributions.

* This limit on annual contributions applies for 2003 and 2004.

Looking forward. The limit on annual contributions to a Roth IRA is scheduled to increase over the next several years. You never know when Congress is going to change the law again, but under current law the regular amount will increase from $3,000 to $4,000 in 2005, and to $5,000 in 2008. The added amount you can contribute if you are 50 or older stays at $500 until 2006, when it increases to $1,000.

Maximum Roth IRA Contributions

	Under 50	Over 49
2003	$3,000	$3,500
2004	$3,000	$3,500
2005	$4,000	$4,500
2006	$4,000	$5,000
2007	$4,000	$5,000
2008	$5,000	$6,000

Compensation or Alimony Income

For each year you contribute to a Roth IRA, you (or your spouse, if you file jointly) must have compensation or alimony income. If you don't have compensation or alimony income you can't contribute, even if you have other types of income. And if your compensation or alimony income is less than the maximum contribution, the amount you can contribute is reduced.

Compensation Income

Compensation income includes amounts you receive from your employer of course, but also includes self-employment income from your own business or from a partnership that generates this type of income. There's a special rule that treats alimony income as compensation income, just for purposes of determining how much you can contribute to an IRA. That means you can contribute to an IRA if you receive taxable alimony payments, even if you don't work for a living. Compensation income does not include investment income, pension income or non-taxable income. See Chapter 8 for details.

Spousal Roth IRA

If you file jointly with a spouse who has compensation income, you don't need compensation income of your own. As explained in Chapter 9, you can contribute to a Roth IRA based on your spouse's compensation income.

Modified Adjusted Gross Income

For some people the most important limit on contributions to a Roth IRA is based on modified adjusted gross income ("modified AGI," defined below). If this number is too large, your contribution limit may be reduced—possibly all the way to zero.

General Rule

The income level where the reduction occurs depends on your filing status. You don't have to worry about these rules unless your modified AGI is above the following levels:

Start of Phase-Out Level	
Single	$95,000
Married filing jointly	$150,000
Married filing separately, living apart for entire year	$95,000
Married filing separately, other	$0

As your modified AGI rises above those amounts, your contribution amount is gradually reduced or "phased out," and eventually eliminated, as explained in Chapter 10.

Modified AGI

Your adjusted gross income is the amount on your tax return before you claim the standard deduction, any itemized deductions, or the deduction for personal exemptions. Your *modified* adjusted gross income starts from this number and makes certain changes. You get to subtract any income you report because of converting a traditional IRA to a Roth IRA, but you have to add back your traditional IRA deduction (if any) and certain tax-exempt amounts.

Exceeding the Limit

Some people aren't able to predict their income. You may be wondering what will happen if you contribute $3,000 to a Roth IRA early in the year and later learn you don't qualify for that contribution because your modified AGI is larger than you expected. In this situation you can avoid penalties if you take corrective action by the due date (including extensions) of your return for the year of the contribution.

Reduction for Other Contributions

The amount you can contribute to a Roth IRA is reduced for certain other contributions:

- Contributions you make to a traditional IRA (other than rollover contributions).
- Contributions you make to a "501(c)(18) plan." These are pension plans created before June 25,

1959 that are funded entirely with employee contributions.

Your Roth IRA contribution is not reduced or otherwise affected by any contribution you make to a 401k plan or 403b plan. (When you contribute to these plans, you're telling your employer to make a contribution in place of your wages or salary, so technically these amounts are contributed by your employer, not by you.)

Q: What if I contribute to a SEP IRA or SIMPLE IRA?

A: Typically these contributions are treated as contributions from an employer, and do not reduce the contribution you can make to a Roth IRA. That's true even if you're self-employed: you're contributing as the "employer" of yourself.

Q: But there's an exception?

A: Yes. You're permitted to make a regular "IRA-type" contribution to a SEP IRA (limited to $3,000 or $3,500, like any other IRA contribution). If you make this type of contribution to a SEP IRA, in addition to any "employer-type" contribution you make to your SEP IRA, it reduces the amount you can contribute to a Roth IRA.

Chapter 8
Annual Contribution to a Conversion Roth IRA

It's OK to make annual contributions to a Roth IRA you established by converting a traditional IRA.

The law is perfectly clear, and always has been, that you can make annual contributions to a conversion Roth IRA. At one time it appeared that Congress would pass a law that would make it undesirable (but not illegal) to do so, at least in some circumstances. Responding to this situation, the IRS warned people not to combine the two kinds of contributions in the same Roth IRA. But Congress never passed that law. In fact, on July 22, 1998 President Clinton signed a law that makes it completely unnecessary to keep rollover and non-rollover money in separate Roth IRAs. For a while there was confusion over this point, but I expect that by now nearly all IRA providers understand that there's no need to maintain separate Roth IRAs if you did a conversion and later want to make annual contributions.

A Small Advantage

When you do a Roth IRA conversion, there's a possibility that you'll want to undo it. Perhaps you'll have an unexpected bonus and exceed the income limit—or you may run into severe market losses after the conversion and decide it makes sense to undo this conversion and try again next year. Similarly, you may want to recharacterize a regular contribution to a Roth IRA if your circumstances change before the end of the year.

You can recharacterize a conversion or contribution even if you've made regular contributions to a conversion Roth IRA. You may have more flexibility in doing so, and less complexity, if your conversion Roth IRA is separate from the one that has your regular contributions.

This is a relatively small advantage that normally wouldn't justify the added paperwork—and perhaps added fees—of maintaining separate Roth IRAs. Yet if you believe there's a reasonable chance you'll want to recharacterize a contribution or conversion, you may want to consider keeping the two in separate Roth IRAs, at least initially. Later on you can combine them if you wish.

Chapter 9
Compensation Income

Learn what counts as compensation income that allows you to make IRA contributions.

You can't make a regular (non-rollover) contribution to a traditional IRA or a Roth IRA unless you or your spouse have compensation income—a term that includes some items that are not usually considered compensation. This chapter explains what types of income count as compensation income.

Reminder: Your IRA contribution or deduction may be limited by other rules:

- You can't contribute to a traditional IRA for the year you turn 70½ or any subsequent year. This rule doesn't apply to Roth IRAs.
- In a traditional IRA, your deduction is reduced if you participate in an employer retirement plan and your income exceeds certain limits, although your contribution is not reduced.
- In a Roth IRA, your contribution is reduced if your income exceeds certain limits.

This chapter is only about the rules defining compensation income. The other rules mentioned above are explained in other chapters.

Overview

For each year you contribute to a traditional IRA or a Roth IRA, you (or your spouse, if you file jointly) must have compensation income. If you don't have compensation income, you can't contribute. And if your compensation income (together with compensation income of your spouse that can be used to support your contribution) is less than the maximum contribution, then the amount you can contribute is reduced. There are three categories of compensation income:

- Amounts earned as an employee,
- Self-employment income, and
- Alimony income.

Each category is explained below. As you read the explanation, remember we are talking here about whether you or your spouse have the kind of income that permits you to make an IRA contribution. When we say alimony income is treated as compensation income, for example, we aren't suggesting that you report it as compensation on your tax return. You should still report it as alimony income—but count it when you determine whether you have enough compensation income to make your desired IRA contribution.

Amounts Earned as an Employee

If you work as an employee, compensation income generally includes your wages, salaries, tips, bonuses, commissions and similar amounts. But the following items don't count as compensation income:

- Pension or annuity income.
- Deferred compensation (payments postponed from a prior year).

- Any amount you exclude from income (for example, certain foreign earned income).

> ▪ People who work overseas can exclude some or all of their wage income if they meet certain requirements. But in that case, they can't use the excluded income to qualify for Roth IRA contributions.

Self-Employment Income

Compensation income also includes the types of income that are subject to self-employment tax. (It includes these types of income even if you don't pay self-employment tax because of your religious beliefs.) You may earn self-employment income in various ways:

- You can be an independent contractor who provides services (for example, as a consultant or a technician) without becoming an employee.
- You can be a professional (such as a dentist or an accountant) with your own practice.
- You can have your own business (not in a corporation)—in other words, you can be a sole proprietor. If you're a sole proprietor, you report your business income and deductions on Schedule C of Form 1040.
- You can be a member of a partnership or limited liability company ("LLC") that carries on a trade or business. In this case, the partnership or LLC should provide you with a Schedule K-1 each year telling you how much income to report, and how much of that income (if any) is self-employment income.

Active Involvement

In any of these cases your income is self-employment income only if your services are "a material income-producing factor." To translate that into plain English, you don't have self-employment income if you are merely an investor. You need to be actively involved in the business that produces the income.

No Investment Income

Even if you're actively involved in a business, you can't include investment income in your compensation income. For example, if you're a member of a business partnership that maintains some investments on the side, the income produced by the investments isn't compensation income. If your partnership doesn't have a business other than investing, none of the income is compensation income, even if you're actively involved.

Net Earnings from Self-Employment

When figuring how much compensation income you have to support your IRA contribution, it's your *net* earnings from self-employment that count. Subtract your expenses and other deductions connected with the activity that produced the income. Also, reduce your self-employment income by the amount you contribute to a retirement plan connected with your self-employment (such as a Keogh plan), and by the deduction for one-half of the self-employment tax.

Loss from Self-Employment

If you have a loss from self-employment, do not subtract the loss from any earnings you have as an employee when determining how much compensation income you have. For example, if you work part of the year as an employee making $6,000, then spend the rest of the year being self-employed with a loss of $5,400, your compensation income is still $6,000.

S Corporations

If you own stock in an S corporation, you'll receive a Schedule K-1 similar to the one you would receive as a member of a partnership. But income you receive as a shareholder of an S corporation is not compensation income. If you are also an employee of the S corporation, your compensation income includes amounts earned as an employee, as explained earlier.

Alimony Income

For purposes of qualifying to make an IRA contribution, you can count taxable alimony income as if it were compensation income. This is a special rule that permits you to build retirement savings in an IRA even if you rely on alimony income for your support. The rule applies only to taxable alimony income, though. You can't include nontaxable items such as child support.

Items Not Included

The following items may not be included in your compensation income:

- Investment income such as dividends and interest.
- Pension or annuity income.
- Compensation that was deferred from a previous year.
- Any form of income that's not taxable (such as foreign earned income and housing allowance that are excluded from income).

Safe Harbor

The IRS recognizes that it's unclear whether some items are "compensation income." To make things easy, the IRS says you can generally treat any item as compensation income if it's included in the box of Form W-2 labeled "Wages, tips, other compensation." There's one exception: any portion of "Wages, tips, other compensation" that's also reflected in the box labeled "Nonqualified plans" doesn't count as "compensation income" for this purpose.

Chapter 10
Spousal Roth IRA

Clearing up some confusion over spousal IRAs.

One of the requirements for making an annual (non-rollover) contribution to a Roth IRA is to have compensation income. As a general rule, your annual IRA contribution for any year can't exceed your compensation income for the year. But if you file jointly with a spouse who has compensation income, you don't need compensation income of your own.

Special Rule for Spouses

If you're married and you file a joint return, you can make a regular (non-rollover) contribution to a Roth IRA even if you have little or no taxable compensation income. Solely for the purpose of determining how much you can contribute to a Roth IRA, you'll be treated as if you had taxable compensation income equal to:

- Your taxable compensation income (if any), plus
- Your spouse's taxable compensation income, minus
- Your spouse's regular (non-rollover) contributions to traditional IRAs and Roth IRAs.

For most people this rule works out very simply: if your spouse has over $6,000 of compensation income and you file jointly, you and your spouse can each make up to $3,000 in non-rollover contributions to an IRA.

Of course this rule doesn't get you out of the other requirements. In particular, if the modified adjusted gross income on your joint return is greater than $150,000, the $3,000 limit for the Roth IRA will be reduced for each of you, and once your joint modified AGI reaches $160,000 neither you nor your spouse can contribute to a Roth IRA.

Who Contributes?

Some of the explanations of this rule would lead you to believe that the contribution has to come from the spouse with the compensation income. That's not a requirement. It's OK if your spouse or someone else supplies the money, and it's equally OK if you contribute your own money. That's true regardless of whether you personally have taxable compensation income.

What Are the Consequences?

The consequences of using this rule to make an IRA contribution are exactly the same as if you had your own compensation income. It's still your contribution and your IRA. There are no special rules that apply to spousal IRAs. The term spousal IRA seems to imply that you've created some special new animal, but it really means just one simple thing: you relied on your spouse's compensation income to make a contribution that would not have been possible based on your own income.

How About a Joint IRA?

We get this question all the time on the Fairmark.com message board. Husband and wife want to have a joint IRA for the two of them. Sorry, no can do. The "I" in IRA stands for "individual." If you commingle your IRA with any other funds, including your spouse's IRA, you disqualify it.

Chapter 11
Phase-Out Rules

The amount you can contribute to a Roth IRA is reduced or eliminated if your income goes above certain levels.

Most people can contribute $3,000 per year to a Roth IRA ($3,500 if 50 or older). But the amount you can contribute is phased out at certain levels of income. That means your contribution may be reduced—possibly all the way to zero—if your income is too high. This chapter explains the phase-out rules for regular contributions to Roth IRAs.

Who's Affected

You're only affected by these rules if your modified adjusted gross income is above certain levels. The level where the reduction occurs depends on your filing status:

- **Single:** If you're not married, your contribution limit will be reduced when your modified AGI exceeds $95,000, and completely eliminated when your modified AGI reaches $110,000.

- **Married filing jointly:** If you're married and file a joint return with your spouse, your contribution limit will be reduced when your joint modified AGI exceeds $150,000, and completely eliminated when your joint modified AGI reaches $160,000.

- **Married filing separately, living apart:** If you're married and file a separate return, and live apart from your spouse at all times during the year, your contribution limit will be reduced when your modified AGI exceeds $95,000, and completely eliminated when your modified AGI reaches $110,000 (same rule as if you were single).
- **Married filing separately, other:** If you're married and file a separate return, and live with your spouse at any time during the year, your contribution limit will be reduced when your modified AGI exceeds $0, and completely eliminated when your modified AGI reaches $10,000.*

Proportionate Reduction

In between the amounts in the table above, the $3,000 limit is reduced proportionately. For example, if you're married filing jointly and your modified AGI is $152,500 (one-fourth of the way between $150,000 and $160,000), the limit would be reduced by one-fourth, from $3,000 to $2,250.

You've probably noticed that the phase-out range is different for singles than for married couples. For singles, the range is $15,000 (from $95,000 to $110,000), but for married couples the range is $10,000 (from $150,000 to $160,000). Don't ask me why, that's just the way it is. Our Congress works in strange and mysterious ways.

---

* Is this a tough rule, or what? You need to have taxable compensation or alimony income to contribute, but your contribution limit is reduced as soon as your modified AGI is more than zero. And if your total income (modified AGI) is less than $10,000, good luck coming up with the dough to contribute to a Roth IRA!

Special Rules

There are two special rules for figuring the permitted contribution to a Roth IRA:

- If the limit doesn't work out to an even $10 increment, it's rounded up to the next higher $10 increment. For example, if the math says your limit should be $1371.50, this rule sets your limit at $1,380.

- Your limit isn't reduced below $200 until your modified AGI reaches the level where the limit is completely eliminated. For example, if the math says your limit should be $50, you can still contribute $200.

Chapter 12
Modified Adjusted Gross Income

Rules for determining your modified adjusted gross income for purposes of IRA contributions.

IRA owners need to know their modified adjusted gross income for various purposes:

- **Traditional IRA.** Participation in a retirement plan maintained by your employer doesn't affect the amount you can contribute to a traditional IRA—but may affect the amount you can deduct when you make a contribution. Your deduction is reduced or eliminated if your modified AGI exceeds certain levels.

- **Roth IRA.** The rules are different for Roth IRAs. Here, participation in an employer plan doesn't affect your deduction—you get no deduction in any event. But your contribution is reduced or eliminated if your modified AGI exceeds certain levels. In addition, you're not permitted to roll a traditional IRA to a Roth IRA if your modified AGI exceeds $100,000 in the year of the rollover.

Finding your modified AGI is a two-step process. First find your adjusted gross income, then apply the modifications.

Adjusted Gross Income

Adjusted gross income ("AGI") represents your total income reduced by certain deductions known as "adjustments," but before you take your itemized deduction or standard deduction, and before you take the deduction for your exemptions.

If you file regular Form 1040 or Form 1040A, adjusted gross income is the last number at the bottom of page 1 (and the first number at the top of page 2). On Form 1040EZ, adjusted gross income appears on line 4.

Q: Are capital gains included in AGI?

A: Yes. For example, if you have a $20,000 capital gain, it will increase your AGI (and your modified AGI) by $20,000. This is true even for long-term capital gains that are subject to special tax rates.

Estimating AGI

To estimate your adjusted gross income for a year that's not yet completed, it's usually best to begin with your adjusted gross income from the preceding year's tax return and estimate any changes from there.

Q: What if I contribute to, or make a rollover to, a Roth IRA, and later find out that my modified AGI is too large?

A: You should be able to avoid penalties if you take appropriate corrective action. For details, see Part VI.

Modifications

To arrive at your modified AGI, start with your adjusted gross income and then add back the following items:

- Any income you excluded because of the foreign earned income exclusion.

- Any exclusion or deduction you claimed for foreign housing.

- Any interest income from series EE bonds that you were able to exclude because you paid qualified higher education expenses.
- Any deduction you claimed for interest on education loans or for qualified tuition and related expenses.
- Any amount you excluded as employer-paid adoption expense.
- Any deduction you claimed for an annual (non-rollover) contribution to a traditional IRA.

Note that you are not required to add back any contribution you made to an employer plan such as a 401k plan. If you are running up against the limit for modified AGI, one way to reduce that number is to make deductible contributions to an employer plan.

Exclude Conversion Income

There's an additional modification that's made only when you're determining modified AGI for purposes of the Roth IRA. In this case you exclude any income you report as a result of converting a traditional IRA to a Roth IRA. Without this favorable rule, the income reported on the conversion could prevent you from making additional Roth IRA contributions—or even disqualify the very same conversion that is causing you to report the income!

> **Example:** You're single and have a traditional IRA worth $120,000 with no basis. Before you decide to make a conversion your AGI and your modified AGI are both equal to $80,000. If you roll this IRA to a Roth IRA your AGI will increase to $200,000. But the conversion doesn't count as part of your modified AGI, so you can still make contributions to your Roth IRA.

Required Distributions

Finally, there's a special rule dealing with required minimum distributions from traditional IRAs. You can convert a traditional IRA to a Roth IRA even if you're over age 70½ and receiving minimum distributions. But in the year of the conversion, you're still required to take the minimum distribution from the traditional IRA, and you're not allowed to transfer the minimum distribution to the Roth IRA. In other words, that portion of the money in your traditional IRA isn't eligible for rollover or conversion.

What's more, for years before 2005, you have to count that minimum distribution as part of your modified AGI. If it throws your modified AGI over $100,000, you won't be able to convert your traditional IRA to a Roth IRA. That rule is scheduled to change in 2005, as explained in Chapter 12.

Chapter 13
Expanded Roth IRA Availability

A favorable rule that will not take effect until 2005.

A 1998 law expands the availability of Roth IRA rollovers. Unfortunately, this law doesn't take effect until 2005.

Catch 22

If you own a Roth IRA, you don't have to take minimum distributions at age 70½. That's one of the reasons you may want to convert your traditional IRA to a Roth IRA even after retirement. (For more reasons, see Chapter 47.)

But there's a catch. If you're over age 70½, you're already taking minimum distributions. Those distributions can push your income above $100,000 so you don't qualify for the rollover. In this situation, the minimum distribution you receive this year prevents you from making a rollover that will avoid minimum distributions in the future.

IRS Restructuring?

What does IRS restructuring have to do with this? The 1998 IRS Restructuring law includes provisions that are expected to lose revenues. To offset those revenue losses, Congress included a provision to permit more people to make rollovers to the Roth IRA. In the long run this may lose even more revenues. But in the years people make these rollovers, they pay more tax, so it counts as a revenue raiser.

Who Benefits

Under this provision, you won't have to count your minimum distribution when you determine whether you qualify for a Roth IRA rollover. You'll still have to take the minimum distribution. And you'll still have to pay tax on it. What's more, you won't be able to roll the minimum distribution into your Roth IRA. But the minimum distribution won't disqualify you from making the rollover, so you can avoid minimum distributions in future years.

Before You Jump for Joy

Why are we yawning? Because the proposal won't take effect until 2005. Maybe that time frame suits you just fine, but for plenty of people that's a good long time to be on the outside looking in. And there's always the chance Congress will do away with this rule before it even takes effect.

We applaud the idea. But because of the delayed effective date, we applaud it with one hand.

Part IV
Guide to the Conversion Decision

Some time ago, the Wall Street Journal reported that only a small percentage of people who are eligible to convert traditional IRAs to Roth IRAs—and who would benefit from such a conversion—have done so. In a subsequent column, Jane Bryant Quinn commented, "That's too bad. Roths can be a terrific deal, for the right people." If you haven't made the move yet, you're in good company. But now it's time to get serious, so you don't let a golden opportunity slip through your fingers. Here's step-by-step guidance in making the decision.

Part IV: Guide to the Conversion Decision

Chapter 14
Conversion Preliminaries

Starting point in determining whether to convert a traditional IRA to a Roth IRA.

Before you get into a lot of detailed issues concerning whether or not to convert your traditional IRA to a Roth IRA, there are a few preliminary points you should have in mind.

Conversion = Rollover

A quick note on terminology: when you're moving money from a traditional IRA to a Roth IRA, the transfer can be called a *conversion* or a *rollover*. There's no difference in the tax treatment, so these terms really mean the same thing. We tend to use the word *rollover* if you make the transfer by removing cash or assets from a traditional IRA and later (within 60 days) contribute the cash or assets to a Roth IRA (a rollover contribution). We're more likely to call it a *conversion* if the money is going directly from the traditional IRA to a Roth IRA. If you convert the entire balance in a traditional IRA, you don't even have to set up a new IRA: it's OK to *redesignate* the existing IRA as a Roth. In any event, you don't have to worry about the difference between a conversion and a rollover because as a practical matter there isn't any difference.

Four-Year Spread for 1998 Only

Roth IRA conversions that occurred back in 1998 received a special tax benefit that isn't available for later conversions. Unless they elected otherwise, people who converted in 1998 spread the income from the conversion over a period of four years. The four-year spread isn't available for conversions after the end of 1998.

If in Doubt, Convert

Every person who is wavering over the decision whether to convert should be aware of the following:

- The only way to keep your options open for the current year is to convert by December 31.

Here's why:

- If you convert by December 31, you have until your return due date to undo that conversion without paying any tax or penalty.
- If you fail to convert by December 31, you've blown your chance to convert in the current year. You can make a regular contribution to a Roth IRA for the current year any time until the return due date (April 15 of the following year). But December 31 is the date the curtain falls on conversions for the current year.

I'm not suggesting that you should wait until later to think through this decision. If you go through an unnecessary conversion and de-conversion, you'll waste time and perhaps pay unnecessary fees to your IRA provider. But if you have a significant amount of money at stake and truly feel you need more time to make the decision, the only way to buy that additional time is to convert now.

Three Ways to Convert

There are three ways to convert a traditional IRA to a Roth IRA:

- You can take a distribution from your traditional IRA and, within 60 days, transfer the money or assets you received to a Roth IRA.
- You can have the trustee for your traditional IRA transfer money or assets directly to a new trustee with whom you've set up a Roth IRA (a "trustee-to-trustee transfer").
- You can have the trustee for your traditional IRA transfer funds from the traditional IRA to a Roth IRA maintained by the same trustee. If you convert the entire IRA, there may not be any actual transfer, because the trustee may simply redesignate the IRA as a Roth.

In each of these cases, the tax law permits you to transfer assets other than cash to the Roth IRA provided that they are the same assets you received from the traditional IRA. The first method involves the most risk because it gives you a chance to miss the 60-day deadline or mess up some other way.

Meeting the Deadline

To meet the deadline for a conversion in the current year, you need to have the money or assets distributed from your traditional IRA by December 31. If you do that, you can complete the conversion by transferring the money or assets to the Roth IRA after the end of the year and still have it count as a conversion for the current year. This approach may help people who are running up against the deadline for conversion—but be sure you complete the conversion in a timely manner or you'll simply have a large taxable distribution and nothing to show for it.

It's Not All or Nothing

Another preliminary point: you don't have to convert your entire IRA. You can convert part, if you want. If your hangup is that conversion of your entire IRA looks like too much to swallow, consider a partial conversion.

Eligibility

A final preliminary point is to determine whether you're eligible to convert your IRA to a Roth IRA. There's no reason to spend time analyzing the benefits of a move that isn't available to you. Two types of people are ineligible. First, you can't convert to a Roth IRA if your modified adjusted gross income is greater than $100,000. For a married person, this means *joint* modified adjusted gross income. Modified AGI includes certain types of non-taxable income but does not include income from the Roth IRA conversion itself. The other category of person who can't do a Roth IRA conversion is anyone who's married and filing separately.

Chapter 15
Conversion Eligibility

Details on eligibility to convert a traditional IRA to a Roth IRA.

Are you eligible to convert your traditional IRA to a Roth IRA? You may as well answer this question before you go through a lot of brain damage to figure out whether you'll benefit from a conversion. The main points:

- If your filing status is married filing separately, you don't qualify unless you lived apart from your spouse for the entire year.
- If your modified adjusted gross income is greater than $100,000, you can't roll a traditional IRA to a Roth IRA.
- You can't roll directly from an employer plan to a Roth IRA. Only IRAs can roll to a Roth IRA.
- If you inherited an IRA from a person other than your spouse, you can't convert it to a Roth IRA.
- You can convert a traditional IRA to a Roth IRA even if you made a rollover within the previous 12 months.
- If you're otherwise eligible, you can roll over part of an IRA to a Roth IRA. But you can't roll only the nontaxable part.

Details concerning each of these points are provided below.

Filing Status

You generally can't convert a traditional IRA to a Roth IRA if your filing status is married filing separately. There is an exception, though: if you live apart from your spouse for the entire year, you can file a separate return and still be eligible for a rollover if you meet the other requirements.

Modified Adjusted Gross Income

You can't convert a traditional IRA to a Roth IRA in a year when your modified adjusted gross income is greater than $100,000. The term modified adjusted gross income refers to your income after certain deductions (but not all) are allowed, modified to add back certain items that are excluded from income.

Q: How does this limit work for married couples?

A: The limit is the same for married couples as for single individuals. If you are married filing jointly, your joint modified adjusted gross income must not exceed $100,000 in the year you roll to a Roth IRA.

Q: What if I make a rollover early in the year but end up exceeding the limit because of unexpectedly large income?

A: You should be able to avoid a penalty if you take corrective action by your return due date (including extensions). See Part VI.

Q: What if I exceed the $100,000 limit during some later year?

A: No problem. The limit only applies to the year of the rollover.

IRAs Only, Please

The only thing you can roll to a Roth IRA is an IRA: a traditional IRA, a SEP IRA or another Roth IRA. (There was originally some question about rolling directly from a SEP IRA to a Roth IRA, but the regulations make it clear that this is permitted.) You can't convert from a 401k or other employer plan to a Roth IRA. If you're eligible to roll a distribution from an employer plan to a traditional IRA, and also eligible for a conversion from a traditional IRA to a Roth IRA, you can accomplish your goal in two steps: first roll to a traditional IRA, then convert to the Roth IRA. But a direct rollover from an employer plan to a Roth IRA is not permitted.

Q: What about a SIMPLE IRA?

A: A SIMPLE IRA can be rolled to a Roth IRA, but only after you've participated in a SIMPLE IRA Plan for the employer maintaining that plan for at least two years. Before that, the only rollover permitted for your SIMPLE IRA is to another SIMPLE IRA.

Roll What You Received

If the rollover distribution from your traditional IRA was entirely in cash, then your rollover contribution to your Roth IRA must also be in cash. You don't have to show that it's the same cash, but you're not allowed to use the cash to buy property and then roll the property into the Roth IRA.

If you received a property distribution from your traditional IRA, then you must roll exactly the same property to your Roth IRA—or cash proceeds from the sale of that property. A rollover is the only time you're allowed to contribute property to a Roth IRA.

Inherited IRAs

Rollovers are not permitted for an IRA you inherit from a person other than your spouse. That means you can't convert such an IRA to a Roth IRA. This is true even if you plan to accomplish the conversion as a direct trustee-to-trustee transfer. If you inherit a traditional IRA from your spouse, you're permitted to elect to treat this IRA as your own. If you make this election, you can convert the IRA to a Roth IRA if you meet the other requirements described on this chapter.

Rollover Within 12 Months

Normally you're not permitted to roll an IRA more than once within a 12-month period. This rule applies to Roth IRAs, too, but with a special exception. For purposes of this rule you're permitted to disregard a rollover or conversion from a traditional IRA to a Roth IRA.

> **Example:** In November, 2003, you took a distribution from your traditional IRA and rolled it to a different traditional IRA within 60 days. In March, 2004 you want to roll this traditional IRA to a Roth IRA. This rollover is permitted if you meet the other requirements for a rollover.

Rolling Part of Your IRA

There's no rule that says you have to convert your entire IRA at once. You can convert part of an IRA if you choose. Unfortunately though, you can't choose to roll only the nontaxable part of a traditional IRA that contains taxable and nontaxable money.

> **Example:** You have a traditional IRA with a balance of $10,000, which includes $6,000 of nondeductible contributions. If you roll $6,000 of this IRA to a Roth IRA, you're required to treat that rollover as coming 60% from nondeductible contributions and 40% from other money.

Chapter 16
Partial Conversion

Why you might want to consider a partial conversion of your traditional IRA to a Roth IRA.

The word *conversion* seems to imply that your old IRA remains in place and is now treated as a Roth IRA. And that makes it sound like you can't do a partial conversion. After all, how can an IRA be partly a traditional IRA and partly a Roth IRA?

In reality, conversion is just a convenient word for the process that moves assets from your traditional IRA to a Roth IRA. The law is clear: you can do a partial conversion. If you do, you'll end up with a traditional IRA and a Roth IRA. This chapter explains partial conversions:

- When to do a partial conversion
- How to do a partial conversion
- Consequences of a partial conversion

When to Do a Partial Conversion

Most people will find that if a conversion makes sense, the best choice is a full conversion. But a partial conversion can be helpful in some circumstances.

Tax brackets. A full conversion may cause you to report enough income to push you into a higher tax bracket. That may not be a big deal, especially if you're moving from the 25% bracket to the 28% bracket. But if you're moving from the 15% bracket to the 25% bracket, that's a pretty big jump to swallow.

You should understand that only the portion of your taxable income that falls into the higher bracket will be subject to the higher rate. You won't pay a higher tax on *all* of your income merely because it pushes up into the next bracket. Still, in some cases it will make sense to limit your rollover to the amount that you can fit within your current tax bracket, especially if you're looking at the difference between the 15% bracket and the 25% bracket.

Cash available to pay tax. You may have cash available to pay tax on a partial conversion, but not enough to pay tax on a full conversion. If you're under 59½ and you have to use some of your IRA money to pay tax on the conversion, you could end up paying a 10% early distribution tax. It may make sense to figure out how much tax you can handle without dipping into IRA assets and then figure out how much you can convert for that amount of tax.

How to Do a Partial Conversion

Your IRA provider should be able to provide any help you need to do a partial conversion. You'll need to tell the provider how much of your IRA you want to convert. If your IRA contains different types of assets, you'll have to indicate which ones to move. For example, if your IRA is split between two mutual funds, you may choose to move one fund or the other to the Roth IRA, or move part of each.

Consequences of a Partial Conversion

If all of your contributions to your traditional IRA were deductible (or were rollovers from employer plans such as 401k plans), your partial conversion is fully taxable. The taxable amount is determined as of the date of the conversion. For example, if you transfer XYZ stock on December 15, the value of XYZ stock on that day will determine the amount of income you report from the partial conversion.

If you made nondeductible contributions to a traditional IRA at any time in the past, and haven't previously withdrawn the nondeductible contributions, then your partial conversion will be partly nontaxable. The rules that apply here are the same as for any distribution from a traditional IRA. You treat all traditional IRAs as a single IRA, so you don't get a different result depending on which IRA you convert. You add up the total value of all traditional IRAs and also the total amount of nondeductible contributions to those IRAs to determine what percentage of the conversion amount is taxable. For example, if 60% of your IRA balance comes from nondeductible contributions and you convert $8,000 of that IRA, you'll report $3,200 of income from the conversion (40% of $8,000).

It would be nice if you could specify that you're converting only the nontaxable portion. The rules don't let you do that.

Chapter 17
Advantages of Conversion

Here are the main advantages of converting a traditional IRA to a Roth IRA.

What's the payoff for converting a traditional IRA to a Roth IRA? How is it that you can end up wealthier by paying tax sooner?

The answer varies depending on your situation. Some people will receive one type of benefit, others will receive a different kind. Some people won't benefit at all. Here's a summary of the benefits of converting.

A Bigger IRA

A Roth IRA is bigger than a traditional IRA that has the same balance. Suppose you have a Roth IRA with a $10,000 balance. If you meet all the rules, you won't pay tax when you withdraw that $10,000, and all the earnings it generates. Compare a traditional IRA with the same balance. When you withdraw that $10,000 you'll pay a fraction of that amount to the IRS. You'll also hand over a fraction of all the earnings. It's as if the IRS owns part of your traditional IRA and gets a share of all the earnings it produces.

The size of the fraction depends on your tax bracket. The higher your tax bracket during the period you make the withdrawals, the smaller your share of the IRA. If your combined federal and state tax rate is 33%, a Roth IRA is effectively 50% larger than a traditional IRA with the same balance!

You won't get the full benefit of the larger Roth IRA if you don't maximize the dollars you contribute. In particular, you'll lose some or all of this benefit if you use money from the IRA to pay the tax on the conversion.

Avoid Minimum Distributions

This is another benefit that can produce huge tax savings and permit you to accumulate much greater wealth in your later years. Rules for the traditional IRA require you to begin receiving minimum distributions when you turn 70½. If you don't need those distributions—perhaps you can live on other savings, or you have a pension in addition to your IRA—the minimum distribution rules serve no purpose other than to reduce your tax benefits from the IRA.

The minimum distribution rules don't apply to a Roth IRA until after the owner dies. A Roth IRA owner who survives well past age 70½ may leave a much greater amount of wealth to children or other beneficiaries as a result of this rule. For this reason, a Roth IRA conversion can pay off handsomely even if you need to use IRA assets to pay the conversion tax and therefore don't get the benefit of having a "larger" IRA as described earlier.

Reduce Estate Tax

If you have enough wealth to be concerned about the estate tax, you should consider the benefit of a Roth IRA conversion in this connection. The estate tax applies to your total assets at death, including assets held in a traditional IRA or a Roth IRA. The difference is that the estate tax doesn't "notice" that the Roth IRA is effectively bigger. So the amount of estate tax on a $500,000 IRA is the same whether it's a traditional IRA or a Roth IRA.

Consider how this plays out for your beneficiaries. If they receive a traditional IRA, they'll have to pay tax on the amounts they withdraw. The value of what you transfer to them is reduced by the amount of the taxes. But if they receive a Roth IRA, they get to keep the amounts they withdraw.

What it boils down to is that you've reduced the size of your estate—by prepaying the tax on your IRA—without reducing the value of your estate. Most people don't have enough wealth to be concerned with estate tax. For those who do, the rates are very high, and this benefit of the Roth IRA can be significant.

Rate Shifting

The fourth possible financial advantage of converting to the Roth IRA is rate shifting. The idea is to pay tax when your rates are low instead of when they are high. This benefit isn't available to most people, and many people will find that rate shifting works to their detriment.

Suppose you're in the 15% tax bracket now, but expect to be in a higher tax bracket when you withdraw money from your IRA. If you convert to a Roth IRA when your tax bracket is low, you'll pay tax at your current, low tax bracket. Later, when you take money out of your Roth IRA, you won't pay any tax, avoiding the higher rates that apply at that time.

This type of thinking makes the Roth IRA seem like a good deal for young people with very low incomes, either because they're still in school or just starting out in their careers. The tax on the conversion is very low, and it's very possible that a higher tax will apply later when the money is withdrawn.

The opposite is true for people who are in their prime earning years and expect to be in a lower tax bracket when they're drawing on their IRAs. The difference between the 28% bracket and the 25% bracket isn't enough to worry about in most cases. On the other hand, if you're close to retirement and expect your tax bracket to drop from 25% to 15%, you might think twice about converting now. You'll have to consider whether the other benefits can outweigh this unfavorable rate shift.

Don't place too much emphasis on projections that go far out into the future. In recent decades, tax rates have changed about once every four years. If you're 40 and making assumptions about tax rates when you retire at 62, at best you're making an educated guess.

Flexibility

There's a non-financial benefit of the Roth IRA over the traditional IRA. You have greater flexibility to withdraw money from a Roth IRA before age 59½ without paying penalties. There's no way to place a value on this flexibility, so it doesn't show up in financial projections, but it could turn out to be very valuable.

Bear in mind that this benefit appears only after you've satisfied the five-year requirement for your conversion. For conversions occurring in 2003, the requirement is satisfied on January 1, 2008. Beginning on that date, you can withdraw the conversion amount (plus any regular contributions, but not earnings) without paying any tax or penalty even though you're under 59½.

In recent years the rules for receiving distributions without paying the 10% early distribution penalty have been liberalized. There are a number of situations now where you can use your IRA before age 59½ without paying a penalty, including certain medical expenses, educational expenses and purchase of your first home. Yet each of these rules comes with various limitations, and there are situations where people have a genuine need for money without qualifying under any of these rules. You're best off if you can avoid using your IRA before retirement, but if you have to tap it, you'll be a lot happier if you can do so without paying a 10% penalty.

Chapter 18
Disadvantages of Conversion

Converting a traditional IRA to a Roth IRA isn't always a good idea.

Many people are excited about the benefits of converting to a Roth IRA. Yet even the most enthusiastic supporters of Roth IRAs will admit that there are situations where conversion is not a good idea.

A Non-Disadvantage?

Before we get into the main disadvantages, let's look at one issue that's sometimes mentioned incorrectly.

Here's one of the key principles of tax planning: other things being equal, it's better to pay taxes later than to pay taxes sooner. For example, if you can delay selling stock at a gain until the following year, you'll delay paying tax on that gain and continue to invest the pre-tax amount, not the after-tax amount. Some people have suggested that converting to a Roth IRA is bad tax planning because it means paying taxes sooner than necessary.

When you move money to a Roth IRA, you have an opportunity to avoid ever paying tax on the future income and gain earned by that money. The sooner you move to a Roth IRA, the greater the amount of earnings that will be tax-free. Other things being equal, the benefit of getting a greater amount of earnings tax-free precisely offsets the detriment of paying taxes sooner. Naturally, if you have a choice between converting in December of one year of January of the next year, there may be an advantage in waiting so you can pay the conversion tax a year later. Overall, though, the fact that conversion requires you to pay tax now rather than when you withdraw money in retirement does not create a detriment, because of the offsetting benefit of completely eliminating tax on earnings in the Roth IRA.

Rate Shifting

A key potential disadvantage of converting a Roth IRA is rate shifting. This means paying conversion tax at a higher rate than you would have paid if you left the money in your traditional IRA and withdrew it later. This is a genuine possibility for many people who are in their prime earning years now and expect to be in a lower tax bracket when they retire. It's also an issue for people who are converting very large IRAs, because of the great likelihood that the conversion income will push them into a higher tax bracket.

The issue is most important for people who are close to retirement. Tax rates change quite frequently, so it's dangerous to predict what they might be more than a few years from now. I'm inclined to discount this issue altogether if you're not planning to use your IRA within the next 20 years. Also, in most cases I would expect the advantages of the Roth IRA to outweigh a small rate shift, such as the difference between the 25% tax bracket and the 28% tax bracket.

- If you're close to retirement and expect your tax bracket to drop significantly (say, from 25% to 15%), think twice before converting to a Roth IRA.

Tax Payment Problems

Apart from the possibility of an unfavorable rate shift, the main indication that a conversion may not be appropriate is a problem in paying the conversion tax. This is especially true if you may have to withdraw IRA money to pay the tax, and be stuck paying the 10% early distribution tax.

Other Disadvantages

Other potential disadvantages of converting to a Roth IRA are difficult to quantify but worth mentioning in case they may be significant to you:

- *Creditor protection.* Initially at least, the laws of some states were unclear as to whether they provide the same level of protection from creditors for a Roth IRA as for traditional IRAs. Check this out if it's a concern.

- *State taxation.* Does your state follow federal law regarding tax treatment of the Roth IRA? As far as we know they all have decided to do so, but you may want to check this out, too.

- *Flexibility as a disadvantage.* One of the advantages of the Roth IRA is that it's easier to lay your hands on the money before age 59½. This can be a disadvantage if it encourages you to withdraw funds you should have left untouched until retirement.

Chapter 19
Conversion Consequences

Answers to questions about the consequences of converting a traditional IRA to a Roth IRA.

Unlike other IRA rollovers, a conversion or rollover from a traditional IRA to a Roth IRA is taxable. All of the income is treated as ordinary income, even if some or all of the income received by your IRA was capital gain.

Amount Taxable

If all of your contributions to all of your traditional IRAs have been deductible, then the full amount of your rollover is taxable.

Q: Can I report part of the income as capital gain?

A: No, it's all ordinary income, even if some or all of the income produced by your traditional IRA was from capital gains.

Q: If I roll property (instead of cash) from my traditional IRA to a Roth IRA, what is the amount of the rollover?

A: The amount of the rollover is the amount of cash plus the fair market value of the property, as of the date of the rollover distribution. For publicly traded stock, the fair market value is the average of the high and low quoted selling prices for the date of the rollover distribution.

If you've made nondeductible contributions to one or more traditional IRAs, then part of the rollover distribution will be nontaxable.

Q: Can I roll just the nontaxable part, and leave the taxable part in my traditional IRA?

A: No, your rollover distribution will be treated as partly taxable and partly nontaxable, even if you try to roll only the nontaxable part.

Q: What if I have more than one traditional IRA? Can I roll one but not the other?

A: Yes, but when you determine how much of your rollover distribution is taxable, you're required to treat all of the IRAs as if they were one big IRA, so you don't get any advantage if you take the distribution out of the IRA that has the most nondeductible contributions.

Q: How do I determine how much of my distribution is nontaxable if I made nondeductible contributions to one or more of my traditional IRAs?

A: If you roll over the entire amount of all traditional IRAs you own, then the non-taxable part of your rollover distribution is simply the total amount of nondeductible contributions you made to all of those IRAs, less the amount of nontaxable distributions you received in the past.

If you convert only part of your traditional IRA, or if you have more than one traditional IRA and don't convert all of them, then the nontaxable part of your rollover distribution will be determined by a formula. The nontaxable percentage will be determined by the amount of your total nondeductible contributions (less any nontaxable distributions you previously received) divided by the total balance of all of your traditional IRAs.

The amount of tax you pay depends mainly on your tax bracket. But you need to remember that your tax bracket can change if your taxable income increases. For example, if you are near the top of the 15% tax bracket before you make a rollover to a Roth IRA, you may find that most of the income from the rollover is taxed at the 25% rate.

No Penalty

Normally if you take a taxable distribution from an IRA before age 59½, you pay a 10% early distribution penalty unless you can fit within various specific exceptions. A special exception has been created for qualified rollovers to Roth IRAs, so you won't pay a penalty on your rollover even if you're under age 59½.

Estimated Tax

Most people don't have to pay estimated tax if all (or nearly all) of their income is from compensation that's subject to withholding. But there won't be any withholding on the income you report when you roll a traditional IRA to a Roth IRA. It's possible you'll have to pay a penalty if you don't make estimated tax payments to cover some or all of the tax you'll owe on a rollover from a traditional IRA to a Roth IRA.

Depending on your circumstances, you may be able to avoid penalties without making any estimated tax payments.

> **Example:** In 2002 you earn $60,000 and your withholding is enough to cover the full amount of your tax. In 2003 you earn $62,000 and you also roll a traditional IRA to a Roth IRA, reporting an additional $30,000 of income. Although you owe a substantial amount of tax on this additional income, you fall within an exception to the requirement to make estimated tax payments. The reason is that your withholding for 2003 is equal to the amount of tax you paid in 2002.

It's a good idea to become familiar with the rules for estimated payments if you report income from a rollover from a traditional IRA to a Roth IRA. These rules are discussed in our free online Guide to Estimated Taxes at www.fairmark.com.

What About Distributions?

The special rules for distributions following a Roth IRA conversion are explained in Part V.

Chapter 20
How Much Conversion Tax?

Determining how much tax you'll pay if you convert a traditional IRA to a Roth IRA.

No one should make a Roth IRA conversion without having some idea how much tax the conversion will cost. Here are some guidelines for estimating the tax cost of your conversion.

Partial Conversions Permitted

When calculating the tax cost of converting an IRA, remember that it isn't a fixed number. You can manage the tax cost of your conversion by reducing the size of your conversion. You don't have to convert your entire IRA.

Your Tax Bracket

The tax cost of a conversion is determined mainly by your tax bracket. You have to be aware, though, that the conversion itself can move you into a higher tax bracket. You need to know two things: what your tax bracket is, and how much additional income you can report before you move up into the next tax bracket.

Some people worry that if they move into a higher tax bracket, all of their income will be taxed at a higher rate. That's not the case. Only the part of your income that falls in the higher bracket gets taxed at the higher rate. If you are otherwise in the 15% bracket and have $1,000 of income that's in the 25% bracket, you'll pay $250 of tax on that extra $1,000 but still pay lower rates on the rest of your income.

Another Way

Instead of looking at your tax bracket and using percentages, an easier way for many people to estimate the tax cost of a conversion is to pull out the previous year's tax return and figure out how much higher the tax would be if the conversion income is added to taxable income. For example, if the conversion income is $15,000 in 2003, pull out your 2002 tax return and add $15,000 to your taxable income. Then look up the new taxable income amount in the tax tables to see how much higher the tax is.* Of course this method isn't accurate if your filing status has changed or if your income or deductions are significantly different in 2003. As explained below, it isn't always accurate even when these factors aren't present.

A More Accurate Estimate

There are problems with the simplified method described above. It doesn't take into account various ways the conversion income might affect your tax return. For example, this added income might cause you to lose part of your dependent care credit, or part of your exemptions. Furthermore, the simplified method doesn't take into account any differences in your income or deductions.

To get a more accurate estimate of the actual tax cost of the conversion, a tax pro might take your prior year return and redo it, plugging in not only the added income

---

* Tax tables are available online in the Reference room of our web site at www.fairmark.com.

from the conversion but also estimated adjustments for other significant changes. Normally it isn't necessary to go through all the same detailed work you would do in preparing an actual return, but it can be helpful to work through the return, rather than just tack a number onto your taxable income. That way, unpleasant surprises are less likely.

If you used software to prepare your return last year, you may be able to get a pretty accurate estimate fairly easily. Just fire up the software and plug in additional income representing the conversion. Using tax software often makes it much easier to play "what-if."

Chapter 21
Source of Funds for Tax on Conversion

Think carefully about where the money will come from to pay tax on converting a traditional IRA to a Roth IRA.

If you convert your traditional IRA to a Roth IRA, you'll have to report some income and pay tax. How you pay that tax is a key question in determining whether you'll benefit from the conversion. This chapter explains why the source of funds for paying the tax affects your decision on whether to convert.

Other Savings

How will you pay the tax on converting your IRA? The answer I like to hear is, "From my regular savings or brokerage account." Here's why.

The greatest long-term advantage of the Roth IRA comes from the fact that it is effectively larger than a traditional IRA. That's a hidden benefit, because the number of dollars in the Roth IRA is the same as the number of dollars in a traditional IRA. But the dollars in the Roth IRA are after-tax dollars, which means you get to keep all those dollars when you take them out. In a traditional IRA, your withdrawals are taxable. You don't get to keep all of the money you withdraw, and that means a traditional IRA is effectively smaller than a Roth IRA, even when the dollar amount in each is the same.

- Ability to pay the conversion tax from funds other than your IRA is one of the key indications that conversion is a good choice.

There may be situations where your only source of funds outside the IRA is very expensive. For example, you may have to sell a highly appreciated asset and pay a significant amount of capital gains tax. If that is the case, and you otherwise would have avoided reporting that capital gain for a significant period of time, you should consider this additional cost when you weigh the decision to convert your IRA.

Using IRA Money Before Age 59½

Many people have savings in IRAs and not much in the way of other savings. If you are in this situation, you may find that the only available source of funds to pay the conversion tax is the IRA itself.

If you're under age 59½, you'll probably have to pay a 10% penalty on any portion of the IRA you use to pay tax on the conversion. There's no exception to the penalty tax for amounts used for this purpose. You may find that you can fit into one of the other exceptions to the 10% early distribution penalty, but that would be unusual.

In this situation, you have two strikes against you. The first strike is that you're not taking advantage of one of the most important benefits of a Roth IRA conversion: the ability to have an IRA that's effectively bigger. The ideal situation is to end up with the same number of dollars in a Roth IRA (where they are after-tax dollars) as you had in your traditional IRA (where they are pre-tax dollars). If you use part of your IRA to pay tax on the conversion, you're not accomplishing that goal.

The other strike against you is the penalty itself. Stacking an extra 10% on top of the regular conversion tax makes for a heavy load. It will rarely be the case that the benefits of a Roth IRA conversion will overcome this detriment, especially when one of the key benefits, the ability to have a larger IRA, has been removed.

There's one situation where it may make sense to convert even though you'll pay the early distribution penalty on amounts used to pay the tax. Some people have traditional IRAs that consist mostly of nondeductible contributions. Perhaps you weren't able to deduct your contributions because you participated in a retirement plan sponsored by your employer and were above the income threshold. In this situation, even though you're paying a 10% penalty on the taxable portion of the amount you use to pay the conversion tax, the overall benefit of the conversion can outweigh the penalty because the tax, and the penalty, apply to only a small fraction of the total amount in the IRA.

- Unless your traditional IRA consists mostly of nondeductible contributions, it probably doesn't make sense to convert if you'll have to use IRA money to pay the tax and incur the 10% penalty.

Using IRA Money After Age 59½

If you're over age 59½, you can use IRA money to pay the conversion tax without incurring a 10% penalty. In this situation you've lost the ability to increase the size of your IRA, but you don't have the added burden of paying the penalty tax. A Roth IRA conversion can still pay off in this situation, but you have to be looking for a benefit other than the increased size.

One possible benefit would be avoiding the minimum distribution rules that apply to traditional IRAs when you reach age 70½. If you anticipate having financial resources to live without taking the full amount of the required minimum distributions, a Roth IRA conversion may provide a significant benefit. Avoiding minimum distributions after age 70½ is another way of increasing the size of your IRA. If you can leave your Roth IRA alone while you live to a ripe old age, the amount you leave to your children or other beneficiaries may be greatly enhanced.

Another possible benefit would be to reduce estate tax. Converting to a Roth IRA means "prepaying" the income tax on the IRA. That prepaid income tax reduces the size of your estate, and as a result reduces the amount of estate tax when you die. Before doing a Roth IRA conversion for this purpose, you should consult your estate planning professional to determine whether this possible benefit will fit into your estate plan.

Chapter 22
Timeline for Using Your IRA

Think ahead about when you're likely to use the money in your IRA.

Converting your IRA can provide a benefit or a detriment depending on when you use it, so you should consider this issue before you decide to convert.

Less than Five Years

If you're under 59½ and you use your Roth less than five years after a conversion, you may pay the 10% early distribution penalty. There are exceptions for certain types of expenditures, but usually the conversion is a bad idea if you use the IRA within this time frame.

> **Example:** You converted your traditional IRA to a Roth and took the money out two years later. You're under 59½ and you don't qualify for any exception to the early distribution penalty.

In this situation you don't have to pay tax on the conversion amount. You already paid tax on that amount when you converted the IRA. But you have to pay the 10% early distribution penalty. Chances are that you didn't really get any benefit from your conversion. You paid tax two years sooner than necessary and didn't achieve any advantage.

After Five Years, Before Age 59½

If you end up using your Roth IRA more than five years after the conversion but before you're 59½, you may see a benefit from the conversion.

> **Example:** You converted to a Roth when your IRA was worth $20,000. Six years later, when the IRA was worth $25,000 and you're still under 59½, you withdrew all the money to fund a new business you were starting.

In this situation you have to pay tax and a 10% early distribution penalty on the $5,000 earnings. Yet you don't have to pay tax on the $20,000 conversion amount (you already paid tax on that amount), and you don't pay an early distribution penalty on that amount either, because it's more than five years after the conversion. The downside here is that you paid tax on the $20,000 conversion amount six years earlier, without getting the benefit of tax-free earnings because you took the money out too soon. Yet you received an offsetting benefit. Without the conversion, you would have paid an early distribution tax on the entire $20,000. You saved $2,000 by avoiding the 10% penalty tax on $20,000.

Long-Term Savings

Some people considering conversion are saving for the very long term. Perhaps you're 40 or younger, and don't expect to touch your IRA until you retire. In this situation I feel that conversion is strongly indicated if you can pay the tax without dipping into your IRA. No one can predict what our tax laws will look like 20 years from now. Yet over this long period of time, the benefits of the Roth IRA are likely to build up to a very large number.

- See Chapter 49 to learn why it can make sense to convert to a Roth IRA even after you're retired.

Chapter 23
Periodic Payments and Conversions

Converting a traditional IRA to a Roth IRA when you're taking periodic payments.

In general, you'll pay a 10% early distribution penalty tax if you take distributions from a traditional IRA before age 59½. One of the exceptions to this rule is for certain periodic payments. This chapter is for people who are receiving periodic payments and want to convert their traditional IRA to a Roth IRA.

Background

I won't go through all the rules for periodic payments here. The rule that's important for present purposes is one that says your periodic payments must continue for at least five years or until you're age 59½ or disabled, whichever is later. If you don't continue to receive payments according to the method you originally chose, you'll be stuck with penalties—not just for the year you changed your payments, but also for all the past years in which you avoided penalties under this rule.

> **Example:** You began receiving periodic payments when you were 47. Four years later you decide you need to withdraw the entire remaining balance of your IRA. The 10% penalty applies to all of your withdrawals: the big withdrawal in the year you took everything out, and the smaller ones in the

years you were taking periodic payments. If you waited until you were 59½, you would be able to withdraw the entire balance of the IRA without penalty.

This rule raises an issue: what happens if you withdraw the entire balance of your traditional IRA in order to convert it to a Roth IRA? Will you pay a penalty in that case?

Fortunately . . .

The answer is no. The regulations on Roth IRAs say that you can make the conversion without penalty—if you continue to receive the periodic distributions you were receiving before the conversion. The difference is that after the conversion you'll receive the payments from your Roth IRA. Remember, you'll have penalties going back to when you first began to receive periodic payments from your traditional IRA if you alter your payment schedule before satisfying the time requirement.

Roth IRA Five-Year Rule

What about the rule that says you pay a 10% early distribution penalty if you withdraw from a Roth IRA within five years after a conversion? This rule is designed to prevent you from using a Roth IRA conversion to avoid the penalty for early distributions from traditional IRAs. It doesn't apply to distributions that qualify for exceptions to the penalty, so there's no penalty for periodic distributions.

Pay Tax from Other Sources

Generally it's advisable to pay conversion taxes from sources other than IRA funds. When you're receiving periodic payments, you have to be certain that you don't have to use IRA funds (other than the periodic payment itself) to cover your tax liability on the conversion. If you have to take additional money from the IRA for this purpose, you'll violate the periodic payment requirement and end up paying penalties as described earlier.

Chapter 24
The Future of the Roth IRA

Will the Roth turn out to be a bad idea with future changes in the tax law?

Some people advise caution in moving to the Roth IRA because of the possibility of future changes in the tax law. What if Congress decides to tax Roth IRA earnings? What if we move to a flat tax, or a national sales tax?

Conspiracy Theory

One line of thought is that the Roth IRA is a Congressional conspiracy. Those thugs in Washington are always looking for ways to cheat you out of your money. The Roth IRA is their latest inspiration. We'll get people to pay taxes up front by promising that the earnings will be tax free, your congressman chortles, then tax every red cent those suckers put into Roth IRAs!

I don't need to spend much time on this argument. People who believe this kind of thing won't be convinced otherwise by a rational argument. But in case you're interested in rational argument, I'll offer one in two sentences:

- Politicians place a very high value on being re-elected.
- Turning millions of taxpayers into suckers with a false promise isn't a good way to get re-elected.

Changing Times

There's a softer and more sensible version of this argument. Ten or fifteen years from now, with the baby boom generation retiring in droves and huge amounts of investments tied up in Roth IRAs where earnings will never be taxed, Congress will be desperate to raise revenues. Some form of tax will be imposed on Roth IRAs out of sheer necessity. After all, the same thing happened to social security benefits.

There's no guarantee that something like this won't happen. I think it's very unlikely, though. The policy decision to tax social security benefits was on very different grounds. Congress never enticed people to enter the social security system with the promise that benefits would be tax free. There wasn't a bait and switch. The initial decision was to create a safety net and not tax the benefits; later Congress decided that people at certain income levels should pay tax on part of the earnings. That's very different from reneging on a promise to leave earnings free of tax.

From time to time, Congress has changed the law to cut back on benefits of various types of retirement plans. These changes have generally been accompanied by generous transition rules to protect those who relied on prior law. Similar treatment seems likely if Congress decides at some point to cut back or shut down the Roth IRA.

Flat Tax, Sales Tax

Is there a flat tax or a sales tax in our future? If so, will it reduce rates so dramatically that people will wish they never heard of the Roth IRA?

Politicians have been talking for years about fundamental tax reform. For a while it was fashionable to promise to make taxes so simple you can file on a postcard. A few years back, Dick Armey, who was House Majority leader at the time, vowed to rip the income tax out by its roots. How long can the current tax law withstand this assault?

A long time, I'm afraid. There are a couple of problems with getting rid of the income tax. One is that no one has come up with a viable alternative. Another is that the income tax is woven so completely into our entire economy that it would take many years to switch to a different system, assuming we were willing to do so.

All of the alternatives to the present income tax that have been proposed have different flaws, but most have one major flaw in common: they shift the tax burden from the wealthy to those who are less wealthy in a major way. Cynics tend to believe that wealthy Americans are able to avoid paying income tax, as Leona Helmsley was quoted as saying: "Only the little people pay taxes." The reality is quite different. Wealthy taxpayers use many ways to reduce their taxes, of course, but when all is said and done, the highest income Americans pay a whopping share of the income tax. The various flat tax and sales tax proposals would change that dramatically. When people take a close look at the flat tax, it starts to lose its shine.

One of the big complaints about the income tax is its complexity. But that's also one of the big problems with getting rid of it. The income tax is woven into our economy in innumerable ways. People always mention the millions of Americans who count on being able to deduct their home mortgage interest, and the charities that rely on the contribution deduction to keep donors interested. That's just the tip of the iceberg. There are literally trillions of dollars invested in various types of arrangements designed to provide income tax benefits of one kind or another. Pension plans, rental property, plant and machinery, government bonds—the list goes on and on, and reaches every facet of government and industry.

Change is possible, of course, but a sweeping change of the type politicians sometimes like to suggest would require many years of study just to plan for it, and at least a decade of transition. Notably, for all the talk in Washington about repealing the income tax, Congress hasn't taken even the first step toward developing a plausible alternative.

And there's another possibility the cynics generally fail to mention. Congress could make changes that will make the Roth IRA more attractive. In particular, Congress might close the budget gap with a general increase in the tax rates. People with money in traditional IRAs would pay those higher rates when they take the money out. People who converted to Roth IRAs before the higher rates took effect would receive a windfall. This seems to me a plausible scenario, especially considering that tax rates now are lower then they have been during most of our recent history.

- I don't have a crystal ball, but my best guess is that future tax changes are more likely to be good than bad for Roth IRAs.

Part V
Distributions from Roth IRAs

Other parts of this book tell you how to get money into a Roth IRA, by way of regular contributions or conversions. In this section we explain the rules for receiving distributions or withdrawals from a Roth IRA.

Part V: Distributions from Roth IRAs

Chapter 25
Distribution Overview

The main rules for distributions from Roth IRAs.

The rules for distributions from Roth IRAs are more complicated than we would like them to be. In this chapter we provide a brief overview of those rules so you can get the general idea of how they work.

- **Terminology:** When you put money into an IRA, you're making a contribution. When you take money out, you're making a withdrawal, and you're receiving a distribution. The words "withdrawal" and "distribution" mean the same thing and are used interchangeably.

When Can You Withdraw?

You can withdraw money from a Roth IRA at any time. In some cases you will pay tax or penalty if you withdraw money too soon, but the tax law never prohibits you from taking money out of the IRA. If you really need to take the money out, you can—unless some other situation, such as an order of a divorce court, prevents you from doing so.

When *Must* You Withdraw?

If you own a traditional IRA, you're required to begin taking distributions at age 70½. This rule doesn't apply to Roth IRAs. You're never required to take distributions from your own Roth IRA. But your beneficiaries may be required to take distributions after your death.

Which Dollars First?

Your Roth IRA may contain dollars from different sources: regular contributions, conversion contributions, and investment earnings. These amounts may get different tax treatment when you take them out, so it's important to know which dollars come out first.

> ▪ **Note:** The description below assumes you have not made any excess contributions to a Roth IRA. Special rules that apply in that situation are described in Part VI.

Treat All as One

In applying these rules, treat all Roth IRAs as one IRA. You can't change the order of distributions by withdrawing from different Roth IRAs. For example, if you made one or more annual contributions to a Roth IRA, the first dollars you withdraw from *any* Roth IRA will be treated as a distribution of your annual contributions—even if you take the withdrawal from a different Roth IRA created by conversion of a traditional IRA, and you never made any annual contributions to this Roth IRA.

Add up the amounts in all your Roth IRAs and determine the amounts in the relevant categories set forth below.

Annual Contributions First

The first dollars that come out of your Roth IRA—any Roth IRA you own—will be treated as a return of your annual contributions. That's good, because your annual contributions come out free from any tax or penalty.

> **Example:** Suppose you have a conversion Roth IRA, and you've also made an annual contribution of $2,000 to a non-conversion Roth IRA. You want to take a withdrawal, and you prefer to take it from the conversion Roth IRA because the investments there are more liquid. No problem! The first $2,000 you take from any Roth IRA will be a return of your annual contribution.

Next: Conversions

After you take out the entire amount of your annual contributions, the next dollars that come out are conversion contributions. Again, this is generally a favorable rule. Although it's possible you'll incur some penalty on these distributions, you don't incur any additional income tax because you paid the tax at the time of the conversion. There is just one twist: if your conversion was partly taxable and partly non-taxable, the rules say the taxable part comes out first. This is relevant only if you withdraw your money at a time when the 10% early distribution penalty applies.

Last: Earnings

Finally, you're dipping into earnings. The total amount you've withdrawn from all your Roth IRAs is greater than the total amount of annual contributions and conversion contributions. If you meet certain requirements, you can take the earnings entirely free of tax. See Chapter 27. If you don't meet those requirements, you'll need to pay tax—and possibly an early distribution penalty—when you make this withdrawal. See Chapter 29.

Treatment of Distributions

The tax treatment of the different categories of distributions may be summarized as follows:

Annual Contributions

These amounts can be withdrawn at any time with no tax and no penalty.

Taxable Portion of a Conversion

You dip into this category only when the lifetime total of withdrawals from all Roth IRAs exceeds the lifetime total of annual contributions to Roth IRAs. You pay no tax on these distributions because you paid tax at the time of the conversion. But when these amounts are withdrawn before the first day of the fifth year after the year of the conversion, but you're subject to 10% early withdrawal penalty if you're under age 59½ unless an exception applies.

Beginning on the first day of the fifth year after the year of the conversion these amounts can be withdrawn at any time with no tax and no penalty.

Nontaxable Portion of Any Conversion

This category exists if you converted a traditional IRA after making nondeductible contributions. You withdraw money in this category only after the taxable portion of the same conversion has been withdrawn. You can withdraw this money at any time with no tax and no penalty—but only after you've withdrawn the taxable portion of the conversion.

Earnings

In a Roth IRA, the term *earnings* applies to any overall increase in the value of the assets, even if the increase in value represents growth in the value of an asset you have not yet sold. You don't withdraw earnings until after all amounts other than earnings have been withdrawn. If earnings are withdrawn before the first day of the fifth year after the year you first established a Roth IRA, they are taxable as ordinary income, and also subject to the 10% early withdrawal penalty if you're under age 59½ unless an exception applies.

Beginning on the first day of the fifth year after the year you first established a Roth IRA, earnings can be withdrawn with no tax and no penalty if you're over age 59½ or otherwise meet the requirements for a qualified distribution (death, disability, first-time homeowner). Otherwise, withdrawals of earnings continue to be taxable as ordinary income and, unless an exception applies, subject to the 10% early withdrawal penalty.

Further details, including the definition of qualified distribution and an explanation of exceptions to the early distribution penalty, are provided in the chapters that follow.

Chapter 26
Tax-Free Distributions

Rules for tax-free distributions from Roth IRAs.

In most cases the best strategy is to leave as much money in your IRA as you can, and for as long as you can. But if you need early access to that money, you're generally in better shape with a Roth IRA than with a traditional IRA. You're allowed to withdraw your non-conversion contributions at any time without paying tax or penalty. This is not the case for the earnings, however. Unless you meet the tests described below, a withdrawal of earnings will be taxable—and may be subject to a penalty as well.

Withdrawing Your Contributions

The rules for Roth IRAs permit you to do something that isn't allowed for traditional IRAs: withdraw the nontaxable part of your money first. Distributions from traditional IRAs come partly from earnings and partly from contributions. But when you take money out of a Roth IRA, the first dollars you take out are considered to be a return of your annual contributions. You don't have to meet any special tests to receive those dollars free of tax. You can take them out any time, for any reason, without paying tax or penalties.

When you apply this rule, you treat all of your Roth IRAs like a single big Roth IRA.

> **Example:** Suppose you have a Roth IRA with a balance of $2,500 (a $2,000 contribution and $500 of earnings) and another Roth IRA with a balance of $3,000 (a $2,000 contribution in a different year and $1,000 of earnings). You can withdraw the entire $3,000 from the second Roth IRA without paying tax, even if you don't meet the tests to withdraw earnings tax-free. Your other Roth IRA will now be treated as if it has $1,000 of contribution and $1,500 of earnings.

There's an exception to the rule that annual contributions come first when you withdraw money from a Roth IRA. When you withdraw *excess contributions* (contributions that are not permitted, or contributions that are larger than permitted) you may be required to withdraw earnings attributable to those contributions. See Chapter 33.

> ▪ In a way, you might consider it a disadvantage to be able to take money out of a Roth IRA so easily. Remember, the best way to grow your investments is to keep as much as possible in your Roth IRA as long as possible, so it will continue to earn investment income tax-free. You may find it hard to resist the temptation to take money out of your Roth IRA—and later regret that you withdrew the money.

Qualified Distributions

If you receive a distribution of *earnings* from your Roth IRA, you're required to pay tax (and possibly penalties) unless you received a qualified distribution. A qualified distribution is a distribution that satisfies two tests: a *five-year test* and a *type of distribution test*. It's not enough to meet just one of these; both are necessary.

Five-Year Test

The five-year test is satisfied beginning on January 1 of the fifth year after the first year you establish a Roth IRA. If you established a Roth IRA in 1998, any distribution from a Roth IRA will satisfy the five-year test if the distribution occurs on or after January 1, 2003. If you waited until 1999 to start a Roth IRA, you can't receive a qualified distribution until January 1, 2004.

The five-year test is satisfied on January 1 even if you establish your Roth IRA late in the year. In fact, you're treated as if you established your Roth IRA in the previous year if you make the contribution on or before April 15 and designate it as a contribution for the previous year.

- **Fiscal year taxpayers:** If you belong to that small minority of taxpayers who file on a taxable year other than the calendar year, your five-year test will be satisfied on the first day of the fifth taxable year after the taxable year you established a Roth IRA.

When you meet the five-year test for one Roth IRA, you meet it for *all* Roth IRAs. For example, suppose you contributed $500 to a Roth IRA in 1998. Three years later you decided to set up another Roth IRA and contribute $2,000. Both IRAs will meet the five-year test on January 1, 2003.

Type of Distribution

Even after you meet the five-year test, only certain types of distributions are treated as qualified distributions. There are four types of qualified distributions:

- Distributions made on or after the date you reach age 59½.

- Distributions made to your beneficiary after your death.

- If you become disabled, distributions attributable to your disability.
- Qualified first-time homebuyer distributions.

As discussed later, a distribution of earnings that fails to meet these tests will be taxable, and may be subject to a penalty as well.

Chapter 27
First-Time Homebuyer

Requirements to be considered a first-time homebuyer under IRA rules.

If you receive a qualified first-time homebuyer distribution from a traditional IRA you don't have to pay the 10% early distribution penalty even if you are less than 59½ years old. And if you take a qualified first-time homebuyer distribution from a Roth IRA after you satisfy the five-year requirement, you don't have to pay tax on the distribution.

To have a qualified first-time homebuyer distribution, you need to meet all of the following requirements, which are discussed below:

- The purchase must be a principal residence.
- The person for whom it is a principal residence must be the owner of the IRA or a family member (within limits).
- The person for whom it is a principal residence must be a "first-time homebuyer" (generally someone who has not owned a home in the previous two years).
- The purchase must cover "qualified acquisition costs."

- The owner of the IRA may not treat more than $10,000 as qualified first-time homebuyer distributions (a lifetime limitation).
- The purchase must be made within the applicable time limit.

Principal Residence

The qualifying purchase does not have to be a traditional home. For example, a houseboat may qualify for this purpose, if that's your primary home. But the purchase must be a principal residence. It can't be a vacation home where you or your family member stay for a small part of the year.

IRA Owner or Family Member

You can't use this IRA distribution to buy a home for just anyone. It has to be for yourself, your spouse, your child, grandchild or ancestor, or your spouse's child, grandchild or ancestor. If you choose to help a sibling, or a niece or nephew, the rule doesn't apply.

First-Time Homebuyer

The rule only applies if the person who will use this home as a principal residence is a first-time homebuyer. This is not necessarily someone who has never owned a home. But it must be someone who has not owned a principal residence during the two-year period ending on the date of acquisition of the new home. And if that person is married, the spouse must not have owned a principal residence during that period, either.

Qualified Acquisition Costs

This is a fairly easy requirement to meet. The amounts paid must be costs of acquiring, constructing, or reconstructing a residence, including any usual or reasonable settlement, financing, or other closing costs.

$10,000 Limit

This rule is subject to a lifetime limit of $10,000. It appears that this limit applies to the IRA owner, not the purchaser of the home, if these are two different people.

> **Example:** Your son needs $20,000 for the down payment on a home. For this purpose he will take $10,000 from his IRA and you will take $10,000 from your IRA. Assuming neither you nor your son has taken a previous qualified first-time homebuyer distribution, both distributions will qualify.

> **Example:** Your son and daughter each need $10,000 for the down payment on a home. For this purpose you take $20,000 from your IRA. Only the first $10,000 will be a qualified first-time homebuyer distribution.

When you determine whether you are a first-time homebuyer you must take into account any previous ownership of a principal residence by your spouse. But it appears that the $10,000 limit applies separately to each spouse.

> **Example:** You need $20,000 for the down payment on a home. For this purpose you and your spouse each withdraw $10,000 from an IRA. If you meet the other requirements, both distributions can be qualified first-time homebuyer distributions.

It appears that if you are withdrawing from a Roth IRA for this purpose, only the amount of the distribution that exceeds your previous contributions counts toward the $10,000 limit.

Example: You have $14,000 in your Roth IRA, including $8,000 of contributions and $6,000 of earnings. If you meet the other requirements, you can use the entire Roth IRA for the purchase of a principal residence, using only $6,000 of your lifetime limit.

Time Limit

Your distribution won't qualify if you take the money out of the IRA too far in advance of the closing of your purchase. The payment must be used to pay qualified acquisition costs before the close of the 120th day after the day on which the payment or distribution is received from the IRA. If you take money out of your IRA and then run into a last minute snag that prevents you from using the money within this time limit, you are permitted to contribute the money back to your IRA (or to a new IRA) within the 120-day limit and treat the distribution and contribution as a conversion. The 60-day rule that normally applies to rollovers will not apply, and this event is disregarded when you apply the rule that permits only one rollover within a 12-month period.

Chapter 28
Taxable Distributions

Here's what happens when you take a Roth IRA distribution that doesn't qualify to be tax-free.

The basic idea behind Roth IRAs is to take only distributions that qualify for exemption from tax. Inevitably, though, some people will need to take taxable distributions. This chapter explains how these distributions are taxed, and what circumstances will permit you to avoid the penalty on early distributions.

Overview

You don't pay tax on your Roth IRA distributions until you withdraw earnings, and you aren't considered to be withdrawing earnings from your Roth IRA until the total amount you've withdrawn from all your Roth IRAs is greater than the total amount you contributed to all your Roth IRAs, including conversions. If you meet certain requirements, you won't pay tax when you withdraw earnings. But if you don't meet those requirements, you'll have to pay tax on the earnings you withdraw, and you may have to pay a penalty, too.

Distributions Taxed as Ordinary Income

If your distributions are taxable, you're required to treat them as ordinary income. You can't treat them as capital gain, even if the IRA received the earnings as capital gain.

> **Example:** You contributed $2,000 to a Roth IRA in 2001 and invested it in stock. In 2004, when the stock is worth $3,000, you direct the trustee to sell the stock and distribute the entire $3,000 to you. Result: you must report $1,000 of ordinary income. The result would be the same if you directed the trustee to distribute the stock to you (instead of selling it and distributing the cash).

Distributions Without Penalties

If you withdraw earnings, and the withdrawal is not a qualified distribution, you need to determine whether the withdrawal will be subject to the 10% early distribution penalty.

Withdrawals that meet the "type of distribution" test for qualified distributions are not subject to the 10% penalty even if you withdraw these amounts less than five years after establishing your Roth IRA.

> **Example:** In 2001 you contributed $2,000 to a Roth IRA. In 2003, when you are over age 59½, you withdraw the $2,000 plus $400 earnings. You pay no tax or penalty on the first $2,000, which represents your contribution to the Roth IRA. You must pay tax on the remaining $400 because you didn't satisfy the five-year test. But no penalty applies because you're over age 59½.

In addition to the four qualified distribution categories (age 59½, death, disability, first-time homebuyer), you can receive distributions without penalties if any of the following are true:

- You have unreimbursed medical expenses greater than 7.5% of your adjusted gross income.
- You pay medical insurance premiums after losing your job.
- You receive distributions that are part of a series of substantially equal payments over your life (or life expectancy).
- You pay qualified higher education expenses for yourself, your spouse, your children or your grandchildren.

> **Example:** You withdraw money from a Roth IRA to pay qualified higher education expenses for your child. You pay no tax until the total amount you withdraw exceeds the total amount of your contributions. You pay tax on any additional amount you withdraw, but you don't pay a penalty because you paid qualified higher education expenses.

When Taxes and Penalties Apply

If you receive a non-qualified distribution of earnings from an IRA and don't meet any of the tests described above, you must pay two taxes: the regular income tax plus an additional 10% early withdrawal penalty tax.

> **Example:** In 2002 you contributed $2,000 to a Roth IRA. In 2004 you withdraw the $2,000 plus $400 earnings to buy a new computer. You're under age 59½ and no exceptions apply. If you're in the 25% tax bracket you'll pay $100 regular tax (25% of $400) plus $40 early distribution tax ($10% of

$400). You pay no tax or penalty on the $2,000 that represents your contribution.

Chapter 29
Distributions After a Conversion

Tax treatment of amounts withdrawn from a Roth IRA after you've made a conversion from a traditional IRA.

As a general rule, you can withdraw your contributions from a Roth IRA at any time without paying tax or penalty. But if you withdraw money too soon after a conversion, you may incur a penalty.

Early Distribution Penalty

Subject to various exceptions, if you take a withdrawal from a traditional IRA before you reach age 59½, any part of the distribution that is taxable is also subject to a 10% penalty. Congress was concerned that taxpayers might use Roth IRAs to avoid this rule as follows:

- Instead of taking money directly from a traditional IRA, convert it to a Roth IRA. You pay tax but no penalty at the time of this conversion.
- Shortly thereafter, take the money from the Roth IRA, paying no tax (because tax was paid on the conversion) and no penalty (because the early distribution penalty only applies to taxable distributions).

Example: You need to take $15,000 from your traditional IRA at a time when the penalty would apply. Instead of simply taking it out, you convert that amount to a Roth IRA and pull the money out of the Roth the next day, thinking this gets you out of a $1,500 penalty.

To close this loophole, Congress imposed a special rule. If your Roth IRA received a rollover or conversion from a traditional IRA, and you take a distribution from the Roth IRA within five years after the rollover or conversion, the early distribution penalty will apply even though the distribution isn't taxable.

Example: You convert your traditional IRA, with a value of $20,000, to a Roth IRA in 2003, paying tax on the entire amount that year. In 2005, when you are under age 59½, you withdraw $5,000 from the conversion Roth IRA. The distribution isn't taxable because you already paid tax on that amount in 2003. But you owe a $500 early distribution penalty (10% of $5,000) unless you qualify for one of the exceptions (such as disability or medical expenses).

More precisely, this rule will apply if your withdrawal occurs before the first day of the fifth taxable year after the year of the conversion. The year of the conversion is considered to be the year the money came out of the traditional IRA, not the year it went into the Roth IRA, if those are different years.

As explained in Chapter 26, the first distributions you take from any Roth IRA are considered to come from annual (non-conversion) contributions you've made to Roth IRAs, even if you made them to a different Roth IRA. After that, before you withdraw any earnings, your distributions come from conversions. And they come from conversions in the order in which they were made. So if you make conversions in different years, the earliest conversions will come out first.

There's a further refinement. You may have a conversion that's only partly taxable because you made nondeductible contributions to a traditional IRA before the conversion. In this case, when you start to withdraw that conversion contribution, the taxable dollars come out first.

> **Example:** You have a traditional IRA with a balance of $10,000, which includes $4,000 of nondeductible contributions. During 2002 you convert this IRA to a Roth IRA, paying tax on $6,000. During 2003 you make an annual (non-conversion) contribution of $2,000 to a different Roth IRA. And during 2004 you withdraw $3,000 from the conversion Roth IRA.

Result? The first $2,000 of the withdrawal is considered to come from your annual contribution—even though you're withdrawing money from a different IRA, and even though you contributed that money in a later year. The order of your contributions doesn't matter until we come to the conversions.

The remaining $1,000 is considered to come entirely from the taxable part of the conversion, so the 10% penalty will apply to that entire amount. You can't treat this part of the distribution as being 60% taxable and 40% nontaxable. If you withdraw more than $6,000 of your conversion contribution within five years after the conversion, only the first $6,000 will be subject to the 10% penalty because the remaining portion was nontaxable at the time of the conversion.

This penalty only applies in the year of the conversion and the following four taxable years. For example, if you made a conversion in 2000, the penalty won't apply to any distribution on or after January 1, 2005. Also, the penalty doesn't apply if you are over age 59½, or if you can fit within any of the exceptions to the early distribution penalty.

Chapter 30
Inherited Roth IRA

Rules for distributions from an inherited Roth IRA.

We sometimes see statements like this: "On your death, your beneficiaries receive your Roth IRA tax-free." That statement could be a little misleading. For one thing, the estate tax applies to assets you own in a Roth IRA the same way it applies to assets you own in a traditional IRA. What's more, if you die less than five years after setting up a Roth IRA, your beneficiaries may have to pay tax on earnings if they withdraw them too soon.

Estate Tax

The federal estate tax applies to assets you own at death if your taxable estate is more than $1,500,000.* Roth IRAs don't enjoy any special exemption from the estate tax. If you own a Roth IRA at death and it passes to someone other than your spouse, it will be included in your taxable estate.

There is one way Roth IRAs provide an estate tax benefit. Your annual and conversion contributions to a Roth IRA are paid with after-tax dollars. That means the

---

* This is the dollar amount for deaths occurring in 2004 and 2005. If the tax law remains unchanged, the amount will increase to $2,000,000 in 2006 and $3,500,000 in 2009. What happens after that is anyone's guess.

size of your estate has been reduced by the amount of tax you paid on those dollars. The result is that you have a smaller estate even though the value of what you're passing to your beneficiaries is no smaller than if you had a traditional IRA. (See Chapter XX for an example.) That's why you may hear people say you receive estate tax savings from a Roth IRA. The estate tax savings come from the fact that you've already paid the income tax, not from any special estate tax rule that applies to Roth IRAs.

Income Tax

The income tax treatment of a Roth IRA following death is the same as before death, with three exceptions:

- The 10% early distribution penalty generally does not apply to post-death distributions. (Note: it can apply to a spouse who elects to treat the Roth IRA as his or her own Roth IRA.)
- Beneficiaries can withdraw earnings tax-free, even if the beneficiary is under 59½ and the decedent was under 59½—but only if the five-year requirement is satisfied.
- Beneficiaries may be required to take distributions according to rules described below.

One rule that does not change is the requirement for the Roth IRA to exist at least five years before earnings can be withdrawn tax-free. To be more precise, earnings can be withdrawn tax-free beginning on the first day of the fifth taxable year after the year the first Roth IRA was established. That means January 1, 2003 for Roth IRAs established in 1998.

As a result, a beneficiary may have to pay tax on earnings withdrawals if the original owner's death and the beneficiary's withdrawal both occur shortly after the Roth IRA is established. This result isn't as harsh as it may seem, however. The tax only applies to earnings that built up after the contribution to the Roth IRA. Normally that's a small portion of the Roth IRA if the withdrawal occurs just a short time after the original owner established the Roth IRA. What's more, a beneficiary can avoid this tax by leaving the earnings in the Roth IRA for the required amount of time—even if the beneficiary immediately withdraws everything except the earnings.

> **Example:** In 2004 you inherit a Roth IRA that was established by a conversion in 2002. The Roth IRA includes $96,000 from the conversion contribution and $4,000 of earnings. You can immediately withdraw the entire $100,000 and pay tax (but no penalty) on the $4,000 of earnings. Or you can withdraw up to $96,000 (paying no tax or penalty) and leave the $4,000 of earnings in the Roth IRA until 2007, when you can withdraw the balance of the Roth IRA tax-free.

Non-Spouse Beneficiary

If you inherit a Roth IRA from someone other than your spouse, you aren't permitted to make contributions to the inherited IRA or combine it with any Roth IRA you established for yourself. What's more, you have to follow the minimum distribution rules for inherited IRAs.

When you inherit a traditional IRA, the distribution rules depend on whether death occurred before the required beginning date for distributions. There's no required beginning date for distributions from a Roth IRA, so they're always subject to the rules for death occurring before the required beginning date.

For a beneficiary other than a spouse, distributions must satisfy one of the following rules:

- *Rule 1:* Receive the entire distribution by December 31 of the fifth year following the year of the owner's death.
- *Rule 2:* Receive the entire distribution over your life, or over a period not extending beyond your life.

The original owner may have specified which rule applies in the document used to set up the Roth IRA. More often, the choice is left to the beneficiary. If the choice is yours, you have to choose by December 31 of the year following the year the death occurred, because that's the last day to start receiving distributions under Rule 2.

Suppose you choose Rule 1. In this case you can delay your distribution, if necessary, until the fifth year after the year the IRA was established, to avoid paying tax on distributions of earnings. You can also withdraw all amounts other than earnings before that time without paying tax or penalty. When you reach January 1 of the fifth year after the year the original owner established the Roth IRA, you can withdraw the earnings as well without any tax or penalty.

If you choose Rule 2 instead, you may be required to take some distributions before the Roth IRA has existed five years. That's OK though, because you're not considered to have withdrawn any earnings until after you withdraw all the contributions (including conversion contributions). The required distributions under this rule are a small percentage of the overall value of the Roth IRA, so you won't take any distributions of earnings within five years unless you withdraw more than the required amount.

Spouse Beneficiary

If you inherit a Roth IRA from your spouse you can elect to treat it as your own IRA. That means you can make regular or conversion contributions to this IRA, assuming you are otherwise eligible to make such contributions to a Roth IRA of your own. Furthermore, the required distributions described above don't apply to a Roth IRA you elect to treat as your own. You can leave the money in the IRA as long as you want. Note, however, that if you elect to treat the Roth IRA you inherit from your spouse as your own IRA, all the rules apply as if you started the IRA. In particular, you may not be able to withdraw earnings free of tax or penalty until you reach age 59½.

Chapter 31
Rolling to a New Roth IRA

You can move your Roth IRA to a different trustee.

You may find that you want to move all or part of your Roth IRA to a different trustee. Usually the reason is to take advantage of an investment opportunity that isn't available with the present trustee. There are other possible reasons, such as obtaining better service, lower fees or greater convenience. The tax rules permit you to make *direct transfers* any time you want, and *rollovers* once every twelve months.

Direct Transfers

This is the preferred method of moving money from one IRA to another. The cash passes directly from one trustee to another, untouched by human hands—or at least, untouched by *your* hands. That's the key point. Because the assets were never outside an IRA, even for an instant, the tax law treats this transfer as a non-event. There isn't any required waiting period if you want to make another transfer.

> **Example:** You use a direct transfer to move your Roth IRA from a mutual fund to a brokerage account. Three months later you regret the choice, and want to move the money to another mutual

fund. No problem: as long as you use direct transfer, you can move the money as often as you like.

- Direct transfers are sometimes called *trustee-to-trustee transfers.*

Rollovers

The other way to move money from one Roth IRA to another is a *rollover*. You take the money or assets from one Roth IRA, and then (within 60 days) contribute the money or assets to a different Roth IRA. There are two major disadvantages to this approach:

- If you make a rollover, you have to wait 12 months before making another rollover of the same money.
- There's more opportunity for a fatal mistake when making a rollover instead of a direct transfer.

12-month period. The 12-month requirement applies to the money that was rolled over. If you want to make a separate rollover of different IRA money within 12 months, you're allowed to do that.

Example: Your Roth IRA is with a broker and you decide to try out a different broker. You roll half the IRA to the new broker. Six months later the new one is working out so well you want to roll the rest to the new one. A direct transfer is probably the better choice, but you can do a rollover if you want, because you aren't moving the same money twice within 12 months.

Avoiding mistakes. Mistakes can happen with a direct transfer, but mistakes are more common—and more likely to be fatal—if you make a rollover instead of a direct transfer. The problem that comes up most often is failure to complete the rollover within 60 days. You may turn everything over to the new trustee within that time, only to find that the trustee failed to complete the paperwork until after the deadline passed. A failed rollover can leave you in a world of hurt, so make sure you leave a margin of error and double check to make sure everything was completed properly within the time limit.

Why do a rollover? Given these concerns, why would you use a rollover instead of a direct transfer? Some people use the rollover rule as a way to "borrow" from their IRA for a short period of time. You can't actually borrow from an IRA: that's a prohibited transaction. But you can use the rollover rule to take money out, use it for several weeks, and ship it back into an IRA before 60 days have passed. There's nothing wrong with this approach apart from the risk that you'll blow the deadline to get the money back into an IRA. A failed rollover can be costly, so be careful.

Part VI
Undoing Contributions and Conversions

For one reason or another, you may want—or need—to undo a contribution or conversion to a Roth IRA. Fortunately there's a way to do that. In fact, more than one.

Part VI
Undoing Contributions and Conversions

Chapter 32
Excess Contributions

How to handle contributions or conversions that are too large or not permitted.

If you make a contribution or conversion to a Roth IRA that's not permitted, or in a larger amount than permitted, you've made an excess contribution. The law provides a way to fix an erroneous annual (non-conversion) contributions, and erroneous rollovers or conversions, too.

There are various ways you could find yourself with an excess contribution to a Roth IRA:

- The total amount of your annual contributions to one or more Roth IRAs and traditional IRAs for one year exceed the maximum allowed for that year.
- Your total annual contributions to Roth IRAs exceed your taxable compensation income for the year.
- Your permitted contribution was reduced or eliminated because of the size of your modified adjusted gross income.
- Your rollover contribution failed to qualify because you didn't complete the rollover within 60 days, or your modified adjusted gross income

exceeded $100,000, or you're married and filed a separate return.

Whatever the reason may be, a penalty tax will apply if you don't take action to correct an excess contribution. If your excess contribution results from a bad rollover, you may have other problems as well. We'll take a look at the penalty and other problems first, then show how you can avoid them.

Excess Contribution Penalty Tax

If you make an excess contribution and fail to correct it you're required to pay a 6% penalty tax each year the excess contribution remains uncorrected. For example, suppose you made a $3,000 annual contribution to a Roth IRA early in 2003, then got a larger bonus than you expected and found that your permitted contribution was only $1,800. Your excess contribution was $1,200. If you didn't correct the excess contribution for 2003, you had to pay $72 excess contribution tax (6% of $1,200). And if you left the problem uncorrected beyond the end of 2004, you owe another $72. You'll continue to owe this tax each year until you correct the excess contribution.

Bad Conversions and Rollovers Cause Other Woes

A bad conversion or rollover contribution—one that fails to meet the requirements to be a qualified rollover contribution—is an excess contribution that's subject to the 6% tax if you don't correct it. But you're likely to have other problems if you make a bad conversion or rollover contribution:

- If you're under age 59½ you may pay a 10% penalty on the early distribution you took in order to start the conversion or rollover.

- The tax you owe because of the bad conversion or rollover may cause you to incur another penalty: the penalty for underpayment of estimated tax.

In short, if you find that you've made a bad contribution, conversion or rollover, there are pretty good reasons to correct the mistake before penalties apply!

Corrective Action

There are two types of corrective action you can take if you've made an improper contribution to a Roth IRA. One is to withdraw the improper contribution and any earnings on that amount. The other is to recharacterize the contribution (or part of it) as a contribution to a traditional IRA. In some situations only one of these alternatives will provide effective relief.

Correction by Withdrawing Excess

If you find that your contribution to a Roth IRA was improper or too large, you can avoid the 6% penalty tax by taking the money out. Relief from the penalty is available only if the following are true:

- You receive a distribution from the IRA on or before the due date (including extensions) for filing your return for the year of the contribution.

- The distribution includes the amount of the excess contribution *and* the amount of net income attributable to the contribution.

When you choose this method of correction, you're required to report and pay tax on the net income attributable to the contribution in the year of the contribution, even if you take it out during the following year, before the return due date. The earnings will be taxed like any other taxable distribution of earnings from a Roth IRA, and will be subject to the early distribution penalty if you're under 59½ unless an exception applies.

This method of correction may work well if you made an annual (not rollover) contribution to a Roth IRA and later found out your income was too large to qualify for the contribution. This type of correction may not work, however, if you made a rollover to a Roth IRA and later found out your income was too high to qualify for a rollover. When you withdraw your contribution from the Roth IRA you avoid the 6% penalty tax on excess contributions, but you're still left without a qualified rollover, resulting in additional taxes and perhaps penalties as described above. In this situation you should consider a recharacterization.

Recharacterization

Another way to correct an excess contribution is to have the trustee of your Roth IRA make a direct transfer to a traditional IRA, which can be maintained by the same trustee or a different one. To avoid penalties, you must meet requirements similar to those described in the previous section:

- The transfer must occur on or before the due date (including extensions) for filing your return for the year of the contribution.
- The transfer must include the amount of the excess contribution and the amount of net income attributable to the contribution.

If you meet these requirements, you'll be treated as if the contribution went to the traditional IRA in the first place. And you don't have to pay tax on the earnings that are transferred from one IRA to another. The IRS calls this a recharacterization.

> **Example:** Suppose you contribute $3,000 to a Roth IRA early in 2003, expecting your modified AGI to be less than $150,000 (married filing jointly). At the end of the year you find that your modified AGI is $152,500 and your Roth IRA contribution limit is $2,250. Before April 15, 2004 you have the trustee of your Roth IRA transfer $750 plus the earnings attributable to that $750 directly to a traditional IRA. You're treated as if you originally contributed $2,250 to the Roth IRA and $750 to the traditional IRA.

A recharacterization transfer provides a bonus. Besides eliminating the 6% penalty tax, it allows you to keep the earnings you may have built up during the year in an IRA, instead of taking the earnings out and paying tax on them. And a recharacterization can come to your rescue if you roll a traditional IRA to a Roth IRA and later find that you don't qualify for that rollover. If you make a recharacterization you're treated as if you rolled the money to a traditional IRA, which is a tax-free transaction.

Of course you'll benefit from a recharacterization only if you're permitted to contribute to a traditional IRA. If your excess contribution to the Roth IRA would also be an excess contribution in a traditional IRA you can't use this method to avoid a penalty. For example, if you waited more than 60 days to complete a rollover, you won't be able to fix the problem by making a recharacterization. Full details concerning recharacterization transfers appear in the following chapters.

Chapter 33
Recharacterization Overview

Overview of how to undo a Roth IRA mistake by recharacterizing a contribution or conversion.

You might call it the "oops" rule. You can switch your IRA contribution from one type of IRA to another. It works for regular (non-rollover) contributions, and also for Roth IRA conversion (rollover) contributions. Subject to some restrictions, a recharacterization can go from a Roth to a traditional IRA or from a traditional IRA to a Roth. You can use this rule to recover from a failed conversion, or simply because you changed your mind. You can even use this rule to reduce your taxes by reversing a conversion following stock market losses. Now that's a friendly rule!

Recharacterization

About the only unfriendly thing about this rule is the word used to describe it. For the most part I can do without words that go beyond five or six syllables. Anyway, I don't think recharacterization is the best way to describe what happens. It's really a substitution—or, to get down to a single syllable, a switch. You switch the money from one IRA to another. If you follow all the rules, the second one is treated as if it received the original contribution.

Possible Uses

Here are some of the possible ways you could use this rule:

- *Failed conversion.* You converted a traditional IRA to a Roth IRA in February. In November you learn that your bonus will raise your modified adjusted gross income above $100,000. Or your marriage falls apart and you can't file a joint return even though you're still married. Either way your rollover is no good. This rule allows you to set up a new traditional IRA in place of the Roth IRA. You'll be treated as if the original conversion was a transfer from one traditional IRA to another.

- *Successful but unwanted conversion.* Suppose your conversion didn't fail, but it turned out to be a mistake? You found out later that you didn't have enough money to pay the tax on the conversion. Or you discovered that this added income might prevent your child from receiving financial aid for college. Or you simply thought better of the whole idea. Once again you can set up a traditional IRA in place of the Roth IRA, and the unwanted conversion disappears.

- *Market losses after conversion.* You made a good conversion and you don't want to undo it—but you wish you hadn't done it so soon. Your IRA suffered market losses after the conversion, and that means you would report less tax if you were converting now. Here again you can use this rule to undo the conversion—and then do a new conversion later. If your investments are still at the lower value when you reconvert, your tax cost will be lower. Regulations place some restrictions on your ability to do this, but in the right situation you can still use this technique to lower your taxes.

- *Annual contribution to traditional IRA.* You made an annual (non-rollover) contribution to a traditional IRA and now you wish you had contributed that money to a Roth IRA instead. No problem! Substitute a Roth IRA for the traditional IRA as the recipient of that contribution.
- *Annual contribution to a Roth IRA.* The same thing works in the other direction. Maybe you found out your income was too high for the contribution to the Roth IRA, or you simply changed your mind about which type of IRA will work best for you. Whatever the reason, you can substitute a traditional IRA for the Roth IRA, and you'll be treated as if the contribution originally went to the traditional IRA.

Alternatives

Bear in mind that recharacterization isn't the only way to deal with a contribution you didn't want to make. In some cases it makes more sense to move that contribution to another IRA, and in others it might make sense to withdraw the contribution under the excess contribution rules. But recharacterization is the only way you can rewrite the past, and make it as if your contribution originally went to a different IRA.

Chapter 34
Recharacterization Rules

A closer look at the rules for recharacterizations.

Eligible Contributions

Some types of contributions are eligible for this treatment, and others are not.

- *Yes: conversion contributions.* When you convert a traditional IRA to a Roth IRA, you're actually making a contribution to your new Roth IRA. You're allowed to redirect that contribution to a traditional IRA under this rule.

- *Yes: annual contributions to traditional or Roth IRAs.* If you make an annual (non-rollover) contribution to a traditional IRA and want it to go instead to a Roth IRA—or vice versa—this rule allows you to pull the switch.

- *No: tax-free rollovers.* If you made a tax-free rollover to a traditional IRA, you can't transform that event into a contribution to a Roth IRA. It doesn't matter whether the rollover came from an employer plan or another IRA. You can't change a tax-free rollover into a Roth IRA conversion.

- *No: employer contributions.* You can't use this rule to switch an employer contribution from a SEP

IRA or SIMPLE IRA into a Roth IRA. That includes salary reduction contributions, because those contributions are considered to be made by your employer, even though you made the choice for the money to go into the plan. If you made your own contribution to a SEP IRA (the kind of contribution that's limited to $3,000 or $3,500, depending on your age), you should be able to redirect that money to a Roth IRA, though, because that's not an employer contribution.

When to Act

If you plan to use this rule, the deadline for action is the due date of your tax return for the year of the original contribution, including extensions. (If you follow a procedure described in Chapter XX, you can obtain an extended due date even if you filed your tax return without an extension.) The year of the original contribution means the year to which it relates, not the year the contribution was actually made.

If you make an annual (non-rollover) contribution before April 15, 2004 and designate it as a 2003 contribution, your deadline for making the change is the due date of your 2003 return (with extensions), even though you made the contribution in 2004.

If you withdrew money from your traditional IRA in 2003 and completed a rollover to a Roth IRA in 2004 (within 60 days of the withdrawal) your rollover is a 2003 rollover. Once again, this means the deadline for recharacterizing your contribution is the due date of your 2003 return.

It isn't enough for you to take action within this time limit. Your trustee has to complete the transfer before the deadline. It's best to take action well in advance so there's time to follow up and confirm that the trustee finished the paperwork.

The Earnings Rule

You can't switch your contribution unless you also switch the earnings on the contribution. For example, if you started a Roth IRA with $2,000 in January, but decided at the end of the year you'd rather have the deduction from a contribution to a traditional IRA, you have to move the $2,000 and the earnings on the $2,000 to have a good switch.

If there's a loss instead of earnings, you simply switch the amount that's left from the original contribution. You don't have to make up for the loss with an added contribution. In fact, you're not permitted to do that.

Most people who make a switch will be switching the entire IRA. In some cases you may want or need to switch only part. If you make this choice, you'll need to divide the earnings between the part you're switching and the part that stays behind according to an earnings allocation rule described in Chapter XX.

Consequences of Switching

When you switch a contribution to a different IRA according to these rules, the new IRA is treated as if it received the contribution in the first place. You'll also treat the new IRA as if it had the earnings that were actually generated in the old IRA and transferred over when you switched contributions.

> **Example:** You made a $2,000 annual (non-rollover) contribution to a traditional IRA in February 2003. In March 2004 you decide you would have been better off with a contribution to a Roth IRA, so you switch the full amount, which at that point is $2,300. Your new Roth IRA is treated as if it received a $2,000 contribution in February, 2003 and had $300 of earnings, even though this Roth

IRA didn't exist when you made the original contribution.*

- A recharacterization transfer doesn't count as a rollover for purposes of the rule that says you can only have one rollover in a twelve-month period.

Irrevocable Election

Your decision to treat the transfer from one IRA to another as a recharacterization transfer is an irrevocable election. That means you can't go back later and say you really meant to treat that transfer as a rollover or other contribution.

Example: After making the switch described in the preceding example you decided for some reason you would have been better off if you had simply converted the traditional IRA to a Roth IRA (a Roth IRA rollover) instead of making a recharacterization transfer. Too late! You have to make that choice before you make the transfer.

The fact that this election is irrevocable doesn't prevent you from making subsequent changes in the IRA that received the transfer. For example, if you use a recharacterization to undo a conversion of a traditional IRA to a Roth IRA so the money is back in a traditional IRA, you're allowed to make a new conversion of that traditional IRA to a Roth IRA—subject to restrictions explained in our chapter dealing with reconversions to reduce tax.

---

* If a baseball manager decides to bring in a pinch hitter in the middle of an at-bat, the pinch hitter inherits the count of the hitter who was batting. The IRA substitution rule is sort of like that.

Chapter 35
Recharacterization Mechanics

Steps involved in undoing a Roth IRA transaction.

If you've read the preceding pages in this subtopic, you already know about recharacterization in general. You also know the recharacterization rules, such as whether you're eligible and within the time limit. In that case you're ready to learn how to do it.

Set Up a New IRA

Recharacterization involves switching your contribution from one IRA to another. If the IRA where the money is going doesn't exist, you need to set one up. The new IRA can be with the same financial institution that maintains the IRA that received your contribution, or it can be with a new IRA provider. The important thing is that the transfer is directly from one IRA to another. You're not allowed to take the money out and put it in a new IRA within 60 days, as you can with a regular rollover.

Notify the IRA Providers

The regulations say you have to notify the financial institution maintaining both the old IRA and the new one that your transfer is intended as a recharacterization. Merely transferring funds without this notice won't qualify as a recharacterization. If you're transferring to a new trustee as well as a new IRA, you must provide the notice to both trustees. If you're transferring to a new IRA with the same trustee, you'll only have to provide one notice. The notice must be provided on or before the date of the transfer.

The IRS doesn't have a form for the notice. Your IRA provider should tell you what paperwork is involved. It should include all of the following:

- An appropriate heading, such as: "Notice to IRA Trustee of Election to Recharacterize Contribution."
- Your name, address and social security number. (The Roth IRA regulations don't mention this, but it's pretty obvious that you want these to be on the notice.)
- The type and amount of the contribution to the first IRA that is to be recharacterized.
- The date on which the original contribution was made to the first IRA.
- The year for which the original contribution was made. (A contribution made in the early part of one year can be made for the previous year.)
- A direction to the trustee of the first IRA to transfer to the trustee of the second IRA to transfer, in a trustee-to-trustee transfer, the amount of the contribution and net income allocable to the contribution to the trustee of the second IRA. (If you're switching IRAs without changing trustees, this would be a direction to transfer the relevant amount from the first IRA to the second IRA.)
- The name of the trustee of the first IRA and the trustee of the second IRA.

- Any additional information needed to make the transfer (for example, account numbers, telephone numbers, addresses).

Once you've made up this notice, you can send it to both trustees with a brief cover letter. The letter to the first trustee will say, "Please make the transfer indicated in the enclosed notice," and the letter to the second trustee will say, "Please process the transfer to my account from [name of first trustee] in accordance with the enclosed notice." If there's only one trustee involved, the second letter and notice aren't needed. Keep a copy of the notice with your permanent tax records.

- Regulations require you to give this notice before the transfer takes place.

Follow-Up

After you send the notice, you should follow up with the IRA provider(s) to make certain the transfer was made in accordance with your instructions prior to the deadline. Mistakes happen! When you file your income tax return for that year, check the Form 8606 instructions to determine what reporting obligations you have.

Transfer Before Recharacterization

What if you transferred money from one IRA to another before making the recharacterization switch? For example:

- You converted a traditional IRA (IRA1) to a Roth IRA (IRA2).

- Then you rolled that Roth IRA (IRA2) to a different Roth IRA (IRA3) maintained by a different provider.

- Now you want to undo the original conversion with a transfer to a newly formed traditional IRA (IRA4).

That could be an awkward situation, because you're trying to recharacterize a conversion to an IRA that no longer exists. Fortunately the folks at Treasury foresaw this possibility when they wrote the regulations. These rules say you should disregard any tax-free transfers that occur between the date of the original contribution or conversion and the date you make the reconversion transfer, provided that you transferred any earnings along with the contribution. The regulations indicate that the notice described above would go to the providers of IRA3 and IRA4—but they aren't completely clear on this point. If you want to be completely safe you can send the notice to the provider of IRA2 as well.

Chapter 36
Earnings Allocations

How to allocate IRA earnings when you make certain changes.

When you recharacterize a contribution, you have to transfer the contribution *and the earnings on that contribution* from one IRA to another. If you're switching from an IRA that doesn't hold anything other than the contribution you're switching (and earnings on that contribution) you simply switch the entire IRA. But if you're only switching part of the IRA, you need to know how much of the earnings belong to the part you're switching and how much belong to the part that stays behind.

- An earnings allocation is also necessary when you correct an excess contribution by withdrawing the excess as described in Chapter XX.

Switching Everything

There's a simplified procedure that applies if all of the following are true:

- You contributed the amount being recharacterized to a new IRA (one that held nothing at all prior to the contribution).

- You haven't made any withdrawals (or received any distributions) from that IRA, or made any additional contributions.

In this case you'll satisfy the requirement to transfer the earnings if you transfer the entire balance of this IRA to the new recipient IRA. That's true even if you had a loss. In effect, you're transferring "negative earnings" in this case. You don't have to make up for the loss when you make the transfer—in fact, you're not allowed to do so.

Switching Part

When you switch only part of an IRA, you need to allocate earnings between the part you switch and the part that stays behind. Normally you'll want the IRA provider to do the earnings allocation, because the calculation involves the value of the IRA on the date of the transfer. Besides, they're used to doing this calculation. We provide the following information to help with your planning, and your understanding of the process.

Rules in flux. When the Roth IRA was first created, the rule for allocating earnings was somewhat arbitrary and often produced strange results. The IRS announced a much-improved rule in 2000, and issued proposed regulations refining the improved rule in 2002. If you made a contribution or conversion before 2004 and subsequently recharacterized it, you're allowed to use the income allocation rule with or without the refinements in the proposed regulations. An income allocation that relates to a contribution made after 2003 is automatically governed by the latest and greatest version of these rules. The following description applies to both sets of rules because we don't get into enough detail here to cover the differences.

Allocation concept. The basic idea behind the allocation formula is to determine how much the overall value of the IRA changed during the time the money was in the IRA.

> **Example:** You converted a traditional IRA with a value of $20,000 to a Roth IRA. The money went into an existing Roth IRA you created earlier with other contributions. Six months later you decide to undo the $20,000 conversion. You find that the overall value of the Roth IRA went up by 10% during that six-month period. Therefore you have to allocate $2,000 of earnings to the conversion contribution. The total amount you have to move back out of the Roth IRA is $22,000.

Earnings = Change in Value

In most cases we don't think of a mere change in value as *earnings*. Yet in this case, that is precisely what is required. If the change in the value of the IRA is simply the result of changing stock prices, that change still goes into the formula. It doesn't matter whether you sold the stocks or other assets that changed in value.

No asset tracing. Some people run into a situation where it would be nice to recharacterize the specific assets that were moved in a conversion.

> **Example:** You made a conversion from a traditional IRA to an existing Roth IRA that held assets from previous contributions. In the conversion, you moved $20,000 worth of mutual fund shares. Six months later, when you want to undo this conversion, those mutual fund shares have gone down in value and are now worth only $17,000. Yet the other assets in the Roth IRA have performed well and the overall value is up 10%.

It would be nice to simply move the mutual fund shares back to a traditional IRA to get back where you would have been if you never made the conversion in the first place. I had an opportunity to comment on the earnings allocation rule when the IRS was developing it and I recommended that they make this choice available for situations like this. They decided an *asset tracing* rule would be too complicated, so you aren't allowed to do that. To undo the conversion, you'll have to move $22,000 out of the Roth IRA: the $20,000 you converted plus 10% earnings from the overall IRA. If you move the mutual fund shares (now worth $17,000) back out of the Roth IRA, you'll also have to move another $5,000 in cash or other assets to recharacterize the entire $20,000 conversion.

- Although you have to look at earnings of the overall IRA, this is one situation where you do not treat all your Roth IRAs as a single Roth IRA. The earnings allocation is based on changes in the value of the IRA that held the money from the conversion or contribution.

Chapter 37
Reconverting to Reduce Taxes

A way to save tax dollars if the value of your Roth IRA declines after a conversion.

The amount of tax you pay on your Roth IRA conversion is based on the value of your IRA at the time you convert it. If your Roth IRA went down in value after you converted, it may make sense to undo the conversion and reconvert at a lower value. This maneuver won't recover your market losses, but at least you won't be paying tax on money that's no longer in your Roth IRA.

Any amount that was converted to a Roth IRA and then switched back to a traditional IRA in a recharacterization can't be reconverted in the same year (or within 30 days of the switch, if that's earlier). But there are still some valuable planning opportunities for people who suffer market losses after a conversion.

Entire IRA Converted

Many people, through unfortunate timing or selection of investments, have seen losses in their Roth IRAs following a conversion. They're left in the painful position of having to pay a conversion tax on investments that have suffered losses, with no offsetting deduction because the losses occurred inside a Roth IRA.

For a period of time during 1998, people in this situation were able to undo the conversion, and then immediately reconvert the IRA. Beginning in 2000, the rule is more strict:

> "An IRA owner who converts an amount from a traditional IRA to a Roth IRA during any taxable year and then transfers that amount back to a traditional IRA by means of a recharacterization may not reconvert that amount from the traditional IRA to a Roth IRA before the beginning of the taxable year following the taxable year in which the amount was converted to a Roth IRA or, if later, the end of the 30-day period beginning on the day on which the IRA owner transfers the amount from the Roth IRA back to a traditional IRA."

It ordinarily won't make sense to undo a conversion until you get near (or past) the end of the year of the conversion. At that point you may decide that the post-conversion loss in your Roth IRA is greater than any recovery you can reasonably expect in a 30-day period, and decide to undo the conversion, with a plan of redoing it 31 days later.

> **Example:** You convert your $100,000 traditional IRA to a Roth IRA in February. To your chagrin, the Roth IRA has lost 40% of its value by June. If only you had waited! As things stand, you'll have to pay tax on $100,000 next April, even though only $60,000 of that amount remains in your IRA.

You can still undo the conversion any time until October 15 of the year following the conversion. But you have to wait until the year after the original conversion to redo it, and the time between undoing it and redoing it has to be at least 30 days.

Suppose you undo the conversion in June, after the 40% reduction in value. You would have to wait until January of the next year to redo the conversion. It's possible the investments will recover by then, perhaps even be higher than the original $100,000. You would end up paying even more tax than if you had left the conversion in place!

But if you wait until at least December 1, you can undo the conversion and then redo it just 31 days later. That may not be as good as being able to flip back and forth immediately, but it can still work to your advantage if the market losses are substantial as of that point in time.

- Bear in mind that when you redo the conversion, it's a completely new conversion in the new year. You can't reinstate the original conversion. You have to qualify for a conversion in the year in which you redo the conversion. And if your tax bracket increased from the year of the original conversion to the year of the reconversion, you'll pay the higher rate when you reconvert.

Partial Conversions

If you do a partial conversion, you have greater flexibility in undoing a conversion and (effectively) redoing it. That's because the rule delaying the reconversion only applies to the amount that was originally converted. It doesn't apply to an amount that wasn't previously converted.

Example: You converted $20,000 of a $60,000 traditional IRA to a Roth IRA. Shortly afterward you found that the value of the Roth IRA had shrunk to $15,000. Using the recharacterization rules, you undo the conversion, transferring the contents of the Roth IRA to a new traditional IRA. The same day, you convert another $20,000 from the old traditional IRA. This is permitted because you have not previously converted this amount—even though you previously converted another amount from the same traditional IRA.

In this example, you use a new traditional IRA to undo the Roth conversion. That isn't required, but it makes it easier to be clear that the amount you're converting hasn't been previously converted. The regulation says you have to adjust the any amount previously converted for the net income on that amount, but doesn't give details as to how you should do that. The best way to be clear about this is to use a new traditional IRA for the recharacterization.

Chapter 38
Extended Deadline for Recharacterizations

You can undo certain Roth IRA transactions until October 15 of the following year, even if you did not file for an extension.

If you made a mistake on a Roth IRA—for example, doing a conversion when you didn't qualify, or maybe just when it turned out not to be a good idea—the rules allow you to recharacterize your conversion or contribution. The deadline for action is your tax return due date, with extensions. That means that if you file for an extension to August 15, and a second extension to October 15, you have until October 15 to recharacterize a contribution or conversion for the preceding year.

There's a special rule you can use to recharacterize your contribution or conversion until October 15 even if you filed your tax return by April 15 without requesting an extension.

How It Works

There's a little-known regulation that says you can always get a six-month extension—automatically, without asking permission from the IRS—for any election that can be made on an extended return. The extension runs for six months from the original, unextended due date of the return. For all the people who file by April 15, the deadline is October 15. You can make the election by this date even if you don't extend your return. Recharacterizing a Roth IRA is an election that can be made with an extended return, so the regulation applies.

There's just one eligibility requirement: you have to file your return on time. That means either you filed by April 15, or you filed a timely extension and filed your return within the extension period. If you blow your return deadline, you also blow your chance to use this generous rule.

To take advantage of this rule, you need to take all the steps that would have been required if you had done a recharacterization during the year. See the preceding pages for details. Then you should file an amended return on Form 1040-X. The amended return should reflect any changes required by the recharacterization, including, if necessary, a new or amended Form 8606. Write "Filed pursuant to section 301.9100-2" at the top of the return and file it at the same place you filed the original return.

- **Think it through.** This is a great opportunity to recover from a mistake. But one of the easiest places to make a mistake is when you're correcting a mistake. Be careful in working with these rules, and seek professional advice if you're uncertain how to proceed.

Super-Extended Deadline

What if you discover a problem after the extended deadline has passed? Through the private letter ruling process, the IRS has granted an even longer extension to some taxpayers. They won't do this simply because you changed your mind about the conversion, or because your Roth IRA suffered investment losses. You'll probably have to show that the transaction you're trying to undo never would have happened in the first place except for an honest mistake, and that you took steps to correct the problem promptly after it was discovered.

> **Example:** Your modified adjusted gross income was just below $100,000 in 2002 and you decided to convert your $180,000 traditional IRA to a Roth IRA. In 2004 you discover that you accidentally double counted a business deduction in 2002, so your modified AGI was actually over $100,000. As a result, you weren't allowed to convert your IRA and you're faced with significant penalties for a failed conversion. If you explain the situation to the IRS, they may make an exception for you, extending the deadline to undo the conversion.

This is your choice of last resort for undoing a bad conversion. For one thing, the IRS isn't required to grant your request. It helps to have the request handled by a tax professional with experience in this area, but even then success is not assured. In any event the process is expensive and time-consuming. Expect to pay a hefty filing fee in addition to any professional fees, and plan on the entire process taking months to complete.

Part VII
Decision Factors

Should you choose a Roth IRA for your annual savings? Should you convert your traditional IRA to a Roth IRA? This part of our guide will help with these decisions. Chapter 2 provided a brief overview. Now it's time for the gory details.

Part VII: Decision Factors

Chapter 39
Tax Features of IRAs

A look at the tax advantages—and disadvantages—of IRAs in general.

This chapter covers a few key facts about what makes an IRA tick. IRAs have been around for a long time, but some of these points are still often overlooked or misunderstood:

- *Tax-free compounding.* Everyone knows about this one because IRA promoters use it in their sales pitches. Is it oversold?
- *Conversion of capital gains and dividends.* This is the dirty little secret of IRAs: they convert capital gains and dividends into ordinary income. Depending on your investment strategy, you can come out better using a regular taxable investment account than you do with an IRA!
- *Rate shifting.* Rate shifting occurs when you claim a deduction in a year when your tax bracket is high, and report the corresponding income in a later year when your tax bracket is low. Many people benefit from rate shifting if they contribute to a traditional IRA or an employer plan and leave the money alone until retirement, when they're in a lower tax bracket. If you're in the 25% bracket or higher now and expect to be in the 15% bracket when you take money out of your IRA, you should

think twice before choosing a Roth IRA, especially if you're close to retirement.

- *Deferral.* Other things being equal, you're better off if you can defer paying taxes until a later year, and have those dollars working for you in the meantime.
- *Tax-free earnings.* A feature that belongs exclusively to the Roth IRA is the ability to provide earnings that are entirely exempt from tax.
- *Size of IRA.* An important hidden feature of the Roth IRA: it's larger than a traditional IRA.

In the discussion in this chapter, everything we say about a "deductible IRA" applies equally to any employer plan where the contribution reduces your taxable income, including a 401k or 403b plan. There are important differences between IRAs and employer plans, but they're the same when it comes to the tax features described below. Similarly, the term "nondeductible IRA" includes not only a traditional IRA for which deductions aren't available, but also a Roth IRA if you expect to withdraw the earnings before age 59½ and pay tax on the distribution. When we refer to the tax features of a Roth IRA, we're assuming you'll take only qualified (tax-free) distributions from the Roth IRA.

Tax-Free Compounding

One of the key benefits of investing through an IRA or employer plan is tax-free compounding, a powerful but often oversold concept. We'll look first at why it is so powerful, then look at why it's not quite as powerful as it seems.

The Benefit of Tax-Free Compounding

Suppose you're in the 25% tax bracket and project that your savings will produce income at the rate of 10% each year. You plan to save $2,000 each year. If you put these savings in a taxable account and pay taxes out of the earnings, the after-tax rate of growth is 7.5%. After 20 years you'll have about $93,000 ($40,000 of savings plus $47,000 of earnings).

Now let's see what happens with tax-free compounding. To isolate this effect, we'll assume you put the same $2,000 per year into a regular, nondeductible IRA. That way, you still don't get any deduction when the money goes in, and you still pay tax on the earnings—but you pay the tax at the end, when you take the money out. The money compounds at the pre-tax rate of 10%, and accumulates to $126,000. After you pay 25% tax on the earnings, you're left with $104,500—about $11,500 more than if you had the money in a taxable account. (Of course if this were a Roth IRA you would get to keep the entire $126,000!)

This example shows that tax-free compounding can produce a significant benefit even if you get no deduction when the money goes into your IRA and have to pay tax when the money comes out. The benefit can increase dramatically if you extend the time period, increase the earnings rate, or increase the tax rate (perhaps adding in the effect of state income tax).

Why It's Oversold

Tax-free compounding is great. But it's worth knowing that the benefit of tax-free compounding is also available to some extent in a taxable account if you invest for capital gains. People who buy stocks and hold them for long periods can build value over many years without paying tax on the gains until the shares are sold. Even if you do some trading, with careful planning you can use capital losses to reduce or eliminate capital gains. The calculation in the example above assumes that in the taxable account you'll pay tax on all your investment profits each year, and that's not what's really going on. Tax-free compounding is a significant benefit of IRAs, but not quite as big as some of the sales literature makes it appear.

All IRAs provide the benefit of tax-free compounding, but the potential benefit is greatest in the Roth IRA. There are two reasons: the Roth IRA is effectively bigger (as explained below), and tax-free compounding can continue longer in a Roth IRA because the minimum distribution rules don't apply. The opportunity to maximize tax-free compounding is one of the reasons to favor the Roth IRA—but you won't harvest that benefit unless you take advantage of it by maximizing your contributions and minimizing your distributions.

Conversion of Capital Gains

Here's a point that's overlooked by a surprising number of people who own IRAs: earnings you withdraw from an IRA are taxable as ordinary income. This is true even if the IRA's earnings came from long-term capital gains or dividends that would otherwise be taxed at the special, lower rates. The IRA converts those capital gains into ordinary income—and causes them to be taxed at a higher rate. This fact is more significant now than it was a few years ago with the reduction in rates for capital gains and the new, lower rate for dividend income.

With an investment strategy that emphasizes long-term capital gains, it's sometimes possible to do better in a taxable savings account than a nondeductible IRA from which you make taxable distributions. Of course this doesn't apply to a Roth IRA if you qualify to take the earnings out tax-free.

Rate Shifting

Rate shifting is a potentially valuable feature of deductible IRAs and employer plans such as 401k plans. The idea is to claim a deduction in a year when your tax rate is high, then receive a corresponding amount of income in a later year when your tax rate is lower. Rate shifting is most important for people who are in the 25% bracket or higher while they are working, but will be in the 15% tax bracket when they retire.

> **Example:** For ten years you contribute $2,000 per year to a deductible IRA or 401k while you're in the 25% bracket, getting deductions that save you a total of $5,000. You withdraw these amounts (together with earnings) after retirement when you're in the 15% bracket. You pay only $3,000 tax on the return of your $20,000 of contributions, and get to keep the additional $2,000 in tax savings.

The benefit is considerably less dramatic if the rate shift is from the 28% bracket to the 25% bracket. And there's no guarantee that rate shifting will work in your favor. You may be in the same tax bracket after you retire, and it's even possible you'll be in a higher bracket then (due to investment earnings on a large inheritance, for example, or a change in the tax law). But for many people, rate shifting is one of the keys to maximizing the accumulation of wealth for retirement.

A more limited form of rate shifting is available with a regular, nondeductible IRA. There's no deduction for contributions, but the earnings are being taxed in a later year, so you can get some favorable rate shifting on the earnings. In a Roth IRA you get no rate shifting on contributions—but the best rate shift possible on the earnings: a shift to no tax at all.

Deferral

Deductible IRAs throw another factor into the equation. They provide tax deferral, something that's valuable even in the absence of rate shifting. When you contribute to a deductible IRA (or a 401k), you reduce the amount of income tax you pay in the year of the contribution. You also increase the amount of tax you pay when you take that money out. But in the meantime, you have the use of the amount you would otherwise have paid in taxes. It's like getting an interest-free loan.

Roth IRAs don't provide deferral. But they provide the opportunity to receive earnings tax-free, which can be just as good or better. Nondeductible IRAs also don't provide deferral, and they don't provide the ability to receive earnings tax-free, either. In most cases this means a deductible IRA is better than a nondeductible (non-Roth) IRA.

Tax-Free Earnings

The Roth IRA adds a unique tax feature to the equation: the ability to withdraw earnings entirely free from tax. Of course you need to meet certain tests to obtain this benefit. See Chapter XX.

Here's an interesting point: all other things being equal, the benefit of receiving tax-free earnings is the same as the benefit of deferral. If you eliminate rate shifting, and permit exactly the same amount of tax-free compounding, you end up with exactly the same number of dollars in your pocket at the end of the day:

- *Traditional IRA:* You receive a deduction when you contribute $3,000 to a traditional IRA. You're in the 28% tax bracket, so your tax savings equal $840. In other words, it cost $2,160 for you to make this contribution. The $3,000 grows at a 10% rate and at the end of five years you withdraw the entire balance: $4,832. You pay 28% tax, and you're left with $3,479.

- *Roth IRA:* You put $2,160 into a Roth IRA. You get no deduction, so the cost of this contribution is the same as the cost of the $3,000 contribution to a traditional IRA. The $2,160 grows at a 10% rate and at the end of five years you withdraw $3,479. You pay no tax on the withdrawal, so you end up with exactly the same amount as if you had used a traditional IRA.

This does not mean the Roth IRA is always, or even usually, equivalent to the traditional IRA. On the contrary, most people are better off in the Roth IRA. One of the big reasons is explained in the next section.

Size of IRA

There's one more feature of the Roth IRA that's somewhat hidden: it's effectively bigger than a traditional IRA. The reason is that all the dollars in a Roth IRA are after-tax dollars. The dollars in a deductible IRA are pre-tax dollars. And even in a nondeductible (non-Roth) IRA, the earnings are pre-tax dollars.

If you want proof, take a look at the example in the previous section. We showed that if all other things are equal, a contribution of $2,160 to a Roth IRA produces the same result as a contribution of $3,000 to a traditional IRA for someone in the 28% tax bracket. But of course you're permitted to contribute up to $3,000 to a Roth IRA ($3,500 if 50 or older). When you contribute the full $3,000 to a Roth IRA, you're making a larger contribution than you can make in a deductible IRA. Over the long run this hidden increase in the size of your IRA savings can greatly enhance your accumulation of wealth for retirement. We expand on this idea in the next chapter.

Chapter 40
The Roth IRA Is Bigger

Why the Roth IRA is bigger than the traditional IRA—and why that's so important.

The annual limit for the Roth IRA is the same as for a traditional IRA: $3,000 ($3,500 if you are 50 or older in the year of contribution).* And when you roll money from a traditional IRA to a Roth IRA, you end up with the same number of dollars in the Roth IRA as you had in the traditional IRA.

Yet the Roth IRA is bigger. The reason is that the Roth IRA contains after-tax dollars, which are more valuable than the pre-tax dollars in a traditional IRA. This means a bigger boost to your retirement savings.

How much bigger depends on your tax bracket. But the magnitude of the difference can be surprising. If you're in the 28% bracket for federal income tax, and pay 5% state income tax, a Roth IRA is effectively 50% bigger than a traditional IRA of the same size!

- The Roth IRA's greater capacity is the engine that drives the increased wealth it produces for many people.

* These numbers are in effect for 2003 and 2004.

A Little Arithmetic

Let's take the following example. You own a traditional IRA with a value of $15,000. You deducted all your contributions to this IRA, so the entire $15,000 will be taxable when you take it out. If you pay 28% to the IRS and 5% state income tax, your overall rate is 33% and you'll pay close to $5,000 in taxes, leaving you with $10,000 for your own use.

Now suppose you have a Roth IRA with a value of $15,000. You've met all the requirements to withdraw earnings tax-free. The dollar value of this IRA is the same as the traditional IRA, but the after-tax value is 50% larger because the entire $15,000 is available for your own use.

If you're in a lower tax bracket the effect is less dramatic but still significant. For example, if your federal tax bracket is 15% and you pay state income tax at a 3% rate, the Roth IRA effectively holds about 22% more than a traditional IRA.

The Impact

Of course, moving your money to a Roth IRA doesn't make you 50% wealthier. The only way to get the money to the Roth IRA is to pay more tax in the first place. The difference is that a bigger chunk of your wealth is in an IRA, where all of the earnings will be tax-free.

Let's take an example where your combined state and federal tax rate is 33%. You roll $15,000 from a traditional IRA to a Roth IRA and take $5,000 from your ordinary (non-IRA) savings account to pay the taxes. Now you have $5,000 less in your savings account, but in effect you have $5,000 more in your IRA. To make things simple we'll assume you get a steady pre-tax return of 9% for both your IRA and your other savings. This means your other savings are effectively earning at a 6% rate, because 33% of the earnings go for income taxes.

At the end of five years (the minimum time to withdraw earnings from an IRA tax-free), you'll have a little over $23,000 in your IRA. If you rolled to a Roth IRA, that is what you end up with. But if you didn't roll to a Roth IRA, you pay 33% of that amount in taxes and you also have $5,000 in a non-IRA account that has grown to around $6,700. The bottom line: if you take everything out at the end of five years, the IRA rollover puts you about $1,000 ahead.

Bear in mind that this is not a benefit that grows at the rate of $200 per year, however. We're dealing with compound interest here. After ten years, the benefit is close to $3,000, and at the end of 15 years the difference is more than $6,000. That's not bad considering that the amount you rolled over was only $15,000!

The same principle is at work when you make annual contributions to a Roth IRA, instead of a rollover. The difference is that instead of paying tax on a rollover, you're giving up a deduction for the contributions. The overall impact is the same: your Roth IRA is bigger than a traditional IRA, so you get a larger tax benefit.

Words of Caution

The numbers discussed above come from simplified assumptions, and your actual benefits from using a Roth IRA are likely to be smaller. The numbers are being used to illustrate a concept, not to predict your benefit.

Note also that you don't get the benefit of a larger IRA if you use money from your IRA to pay taxes on the rollover. To get this benefit, you have to come up with money to pay the tax from some other source. And if it's costly for you to come up with that money (for example, you have to borrow, or you have to sell an asset you would prefer not to sell) you have to weigh that cost against the benefit.

And one more point is especially important. The switch to a Roth IRA can backfire if the tax you pay on that switch is at a much higher rate than if you left the money in the traditional IRA and withdrew it at retirement. For many people it's a bad idea to pay 25% or higher on a rollover, or give up a deduction at a rate of 25% or higher, if it seems likely they'll be in the 15% tax bracket when they withdraw the money.

If your time frame is very long—say, 10 years or more before you begin taking withdrawals—tax rates are not much of a factor, partly because the long-term benefit of the Roth IRA will outweigh the added tax cost and partly because no one can predict what tax rates will be like that far in advance. But on a shorter time frame, tax brackets can be a very important factor that could indicate you should limit the size of your rollover—or not make the rollover at all.

Chapter 41
Roth IRA vs. Non-IRA Savings

Comparing the Roth IRA with a taxable account.

The Roth IRA offers the opportunity to receive investment earnings entirely free from tax. If you can take advantage of that opportunity, the Roth IRA will certainly produce better results than a non-IRA investment account.

Yet some situations call for savings to be used before retirement. For example, you may be setting money aside for your child's college education. If so, you may end up paying tax on the earnings you withdraw from your Roth IRA. In this situation you may still benefit from using a Roth IRA—but you may not. It depends on your style of investing.

Tax-Free Compounding

If you plan to invest in a way that produces ordinary income on a regular basis, the Roth IRA may provide a benefit even if you pay tax when you withdraw the earnings. Examples of such investments include bonds, certificates of deposit and money market funds. By using a Roth IRA for these investments you postpone paying tax on this income until you withdraw the earnings. In other words, you get the benefit of tax-free compounding, as explained in Tax Features of IRAs. This benefit makes the Roth IRA a good choice for this type of investment.

Capital Gain and Dividend Conversion

If you expect to pay tax on your IRA distributions, and you plan to invest in a way that produces long-term capital gains or dividends that would qualify for lower tax rates, you should think twice before using a Roth IRA. Any earnings you withdraw as taxable income will be taxed as ordinary income. That means you're converting capital gains (which are generally taxed at favorable rates) into ordinary income (which is not taxed at favorable rates). Depending on how your investments fare, a non-IRA investment account may be the choice that maximizes your after-tax results.

Chapter 42
Roth IRA vs. Nondeductible IRA

Comparing the Roth IRA with a traditional nondeductible IRA.

You can contribute to a traditional IRA even if you're covered by a retirement plan sponsored by your employer. But in this case your deduction may be reduced or eliminated, depending on your income level. If you're choosing between a Roth IRA and a nondeductible contribution to a traditional IRA, the Roth IRA can be a clear winner. Here's the choice:

- *Contribute to a traditional IRA.* Get no deduction when your money goes in. When the money comes out, pay tax on the investment earnings.

- *Contribute to a Roth IRA.* Get no deduction when your money goes in. When your money comes out, it's all tax-free.

If you choose the traditional IRA in this situation, you're electing to pay additional tax without any corresponding benefit.

Partial Deduction

You may find that part of your contribution to a traditional IRA is deductible. In this situation you have three alternatives: the Roth IRA, the (partially) nondeductible traditional IRA, or both.

When to Choose the Roth IRA

For many people the Roth IRA is better than the traditional IRA even if all of the traditional IRA contribution is deductible. If you're one of those people, your decision is even easier when part of your traditional IRA contribution is nondeductible. Make your contribution to the Roth IRA.

When to Choose the Traditional IRA

You should choose the traditional IRA only if two things are true:

- The traditional IRA provides a significant advantage. For example, you'll make your contribution while you're in the 28% tax bracket and expect to be in the 15% tax bracket when money comes out of the IRA . . . and
- The part of your contribution that's nondeductible is too small to matter—say, 20% or less.

When the nondeductible portion of your contribution grows beyond 20%, this choice becomes difficult to justify. You should stick with the Roth IRA.

When to Choose Both

You don't have to put all your money in one or the other. You can contribute to a traditional IRA and a Roth IRA in the same year. If you get a substantial benefit from your traditional IRA deduction, but a significant part of your contribution is not deductible, you can divide your contribution between two accounts. If you think this may be best for you, consider the following:

- Make sure the total amount you contribute to more than one IRA does not exceed the amount you can contribute to one IRA (usually $3,000).

- Don't take this approach if added fees for maintaining multiple IRAs will eat up your tax advantage.

Early in the year it may be difficult to know how much of your traditional IRA contribution is deductible. This strategy is easiest when you make your IRA contribution at the end of the year. But there is an advantage to making your contribution early in the year, because your contribution starts accumulating tax-free or tax-deferred earnings sooner.

- Unfortunately this idea of splitting contributions between traditional IRAs and Roth IRAs doesn't work for rollovers. You can't roll the taxable part of a distribution to a traditional IRA and the nontaxable part to a Roth IRA. But if your income happens to fall in that area where only part of your traditional IRA contribution is deductible, splitting the annual contribution may be the solution that maximizes your tax benefits.

Chapter 43
Roth IRA vs. Deductible IRA

Comparing the Roth IRA with a traditional IRA where all contributions are deductible.

You may be eligible to contribute up to $3,000 each year to a Roth IRA ($3,500 if 50 or older). (These are numbers for 2003 and 2004.) But should you? Some people will do better if they contribute to a traditional IRA. We'll start by examining the most important factor in your decision: the tax bracket effect. Then we'll look at the other advantages and disadvantages of the Roth IRA. The most important features that may make one choice better than the other can be useful in making other choices as well:

- Choosing between a Roth IRA and an employer plan (401k or 403b) for annual savings. See Roth IRA vs. Employer Plan.

- Deciding whether to roll over some or all of your existing retirement savings to a Roth IRA. See Roth IRA Rollover Considerations.

The Tax Bracket Effect

The biggest factor that will influence your choice between a traditional IRA and a Roth IRA for your annual contributions is the tax bracket effect. A traditional IRA may afford the opportunity to claim a deduction when your tax bracket is high, and withdraw from your savings when your tax bracket is low. When that happens you'll never fully "repay" the tax benefit produced by your deduction. It's as if the government made an extra contribution to your retirement savings. This benefit isn't available with a Roth IRA because contributions are not deductible.

The tax bracket effect can be large, small or nonexistent. It can even work in reverse, if your tax bracket is higher when you withdraw money from your IRA than when you made your contributions. Here's how this factor affects your choice between the Roth IRA and a traditional IRA:

- If your traditional IRA contribution is nondeductible, you won't benefit from the tax bracket effect and you should choose the Roth IRA. See Roth IRA vs. Nondeductible IRA.

- The tax bracket effect doesn't help if your tax bracket in retirement will be the same as when you contribute to the IRA (or higher). Choose the Roth IRA in this case, too.

- If you expect only a small drop in your tax bracket when you retire (for example, from 28% to 25%), the traditional IRA wins in the short term but the Roth IRA is likely to prevail in the long run. You should choose the Roth IRA unless you are close to retirement and expect to withdraw your savings shortly after you retire.

You should generally choose the traditional IRA if you can deduct your contributions at the 28% rate or higher and withdraw your savings when you're in the 15% bracket. In theory the other benefits of the Roth IRA may overcome this factor in the long term; in practice the time required for the Roth IRA to win in this case is longer than the period for which reliable projections are possible.

- If retirement is more than 20 years away, predicting your retirement tax rate is pure guesswork. I recommend the Roth IRA for anyone under age 45. The promise of tax-free earnings over such a long period is too good to pass up.

Other Factors

For most people, the tax bracket effect described above will be the most important factor in deciding whether their annual savings should go into a traditional IRA or a Roth IRA. Before you make your choice, you should be aware of four advantages—and two potential disadvantages—of the Roth IRA.

Roth IRA Advantages

The four advantages described below provide powerful incentives to choose the Roth IRA over the traditional IRA for your annual savings. Together, they explain why the Roth IRA is likely to be the best choice unless the tax bracket effect works strongly in favor of the traditional IRA.

Amount invested. In a traditional IRA you receive only part of the benefit of your investment earnings because part will end up going to the government in the form of taxes. In a Roth IRA every dollar is working for you. This is the principal reason some financial analysts have been able to project significantly more wealth accumulation for people who can maximize their contributions to a Roth IRA. If you don't contribute the maximum amount to your IRA this factor is less important.

Required distributions. The rules for traditional IRAs require you to start taking distributions when you reach age 70½. If you don't need the money at that time, this rule reduces your ability to continue investing in a tax-free vehicle. The required distribution rules don't apply to the Roth IRA. As a result, the Roth IRA may enhance your post-retirement investment earnings.

Estate tax reduction. Suppose you have a Roth IRA with a value of $400,000 when you die. Your heirs won't pay income tax on their benefits from the Roth IRA, so the benefit to your heirs is the same as the amount included in your estate: $400,000. Now suppose you have a traditional IRA instead. The balance is $500,000 but your heirs will pay $100,000 income tax when they receive the benefits. The benefit to your heirs is still $400,000, but the amount included in your estate is $500,000. Wealthier individuals can sometimes use the Roth IRA to reduce their estate tax without reducing benefits to their heirs.

Early distributions. No matter how well you plan, you may need to withdraw money from your IRA prior to retirement. The Roth IRA makes this easier because of a rule that says the first dollars out are considered a return of your contributions. You don't pay tax (or penalty) on the amounts you withdraw until you have taken out all your contributions and start to withdraw the earnings. This isn't true for a traditional IRA. If your traditional IRA includes any earnings, your distributions will be partly taxable (and possibly subject to penalty) even if all your contributions were nondeductible.

Roth IRA Disadvantages

When the Roth IRA first came out, there was some concern about state tax treatment of Roth IRAs. Nearly all states have now conformed their laws so that Roth IRA investors are not disadvantaged, but there may still be a few states where Roth IRAs are at a disadvantage.

Another issue that was sometime mentioned was creditor protection. For reasons having to do with the way state bankruptcy laws are written, some people questioned whether Roth IRAs will receive the same protections as traditional IRAs. It would certainly be surprising if the laws were actually interpreted this way, but if you have particular concerns about creditor protecttion, you may wish to explore this issue before converting a large dollar amount to a Roth IRA.

Chapter 44
Roth IRA vs. Employer Plan

Comparing the Roth IRA with your company's 401k or 403b plan.

Ideally you should be saving the maximum amount in both your employer plan and an IRA. But many people find this simply isn't possible. There's only so much they can manage to save for retirement in the course of a year, and they need to decide whether the savings should go into a Roth IRA or an employer plan.

We're talking here about employer plans that provide a reduction in your taxable income for the amounts you contribute. For example, if you earn $60,000 and elect to have $5,000 of your earnings contributed to your employer's 401k plan you'll report only $55,000 of earnings. The effect is similar to making a deductible contribution to a traditional IRA. You should be familiar with the ideas presented in Roth IRA vs. Deductible IRA. This chapter deals only with additional points you need to consider when your choice involves an employer plan:

- Matching contributions
- Access to your savings
- Investment opportunities
- Creditor protection

Matching Contributions

Many employers provide matching contributions when you elect to have part of your earnings contributed to a 401k or other employer plan. Employers have great flexibility in this area. They can choose to match all employee contributions, or only contributions up to a specified dollar amount, or none at all. And they can match on a dollar-for-dollar basis or on some less generous basis, such as 50 cents (or less) for every dollar you elect to contribute. It's important for you to know exactly how your employer's matching contributions work. If you have any doubt, check with your employer or review the summary plan description.

Matching contributions greatly decrease the cost of saving for retirement.

> **Example:** You're in the 28% tax bracket and your employer matches 50 cents on the dollar for the first $4,000 of contributions. At a cost of only $2,880 ($4,000 minus the 28% tax savings) you can have an account balance of $6,000 ($4,000 plus the $2,000 employer match.

Of course you'll have to pay tax on the $6,000 (and any earnings) when you receive benefits from the employer plan. But it's hard to beat the advantages of receiving an employer match because of the leverage demonstrated in the example.

This is why most advisors feel that in a choice between a Roth IRA and an employer plan with matching contributions, you should choose the employer plan, at least up to the point where you no longer qualify for the match.

There may be some situations where you shouldn't necessarily follow that advice. For example, you may have reason to believe your employment will terminate before the employer match will become vested, so that you'll forfeit the matching contribution. Or the match may be very small (say, 10 cents on the dollar) while other aspects of the employer plan make it very unattractive. In general though, it's a good rule of thumb to look to the employer plan first when matching contributions are available.

Access to Savings

Employer plans are both better and worse when it comes to getting access to your retirement savings. On the one hand, you can borrow from many employer plans—something you can't do with an IRA. The ability to gain access to your retirement savings by borrowing can be very valuable, because when the loan is repaid your savings are restored, plus interest. If you had to withdraw the savings rather than borrow them, you might find that there is no way to return that amount to a tax-advantaged form of retirement savings when you're later able to do so.

On the other hand, employer plans generally restrict your ability to withdraw funds while you're still employed—including the money you contributed. You can't simply demand to receive your account balance whenever you want or need it (as you can if you have an IRA). In limited circumstances you may be able to receive a hardship distribution, but you may find that you don't qualify and simply can't get your hands on that money until your employment terminates.

Many people will think of this as a disadvantage of employer plans, but you should consider it partly an advantage. The discipline this imposes to keep your savings set aside for retirement may work to your benefit in the long run.

Investment Opportunities

This is a point that is very important but often overlooked. Many employer plans provide a very limited choice of investment opportunities. Sometimes the employer determines the investments entirely; in other cases you may have a choice among several mutual funds or other investments that don't perform particularly well. This is not to say that you can necessarily do any better with your own choices. Yet there are simple methods of investing (such as investing in a stock index fund) that typically do better than the majority of mutual funds and may significantly outperform your employer's plan. Over the long haul a seemingly small difference in investment performance can make a great difference in your accumulation of savings for retirement.

Bear in mind that you can be much worse off if you put your savings in an IRA and dabble with investments that end up producing losses. And some employer plans offer excellent investment choices. It pays to be informed about your investment alternatives before committing your money to one method of retirement savings or the other.

Creditor Protection

Federal laws concerning retirement savings provide sturdy protection for employer plans from creditors of participants. You may lose some or all of your account in a divorce, but it's generally protected from being seized by credit card companies or other claimants.

The amount of protection afforded to the owner of an IRA depends on state law. Some states provide no creditor protection at all for IRAs; many others provide only limited protection. If the possibility of bankruptcy is a concern, you should determine the kind of protection your state provides to IRAs before choosing an IRA over an employer plan for your retirement savings.

Chapter 45
Tax on Social Security

How using a Roth IRA affects the amount of tax you pay on social security benefits.

If your income is above certain levels you have to pay tax on a portion of your social security benefit. Certain forms of exempt income are included when you determine how much of your social security benefit is taxable. Nontaxable distributions from a Roth IRA won't affect the tax on your social security benefits, however.

Nontaxable Distributions

When Congress decided how much tax people should pay on social security benefits, the general idea was that people with higher incomes should pay tax on a bigger portion of the benefit. It seemed fair (to the lawmakers, at least) to include certain types of nontaxable income for this purpose. So when you determine how much of your social security benefit is taxable you have to include the following items:

- Tax-exempt interest
- Series EE bond income that's excluded under the education savings bond program
- Certain otherwise excluded income earned abroad

Some people use a shorthand description of this rule, saying you have to include "tax-exempt income" when you figure how much of your social security benefit is taxable. You might wonder, then, if tax-exempt distributions from Roth IRAs would affect the calculation.

The answer is *no*. The only forms of tax-exempt income that affect the tax on your social security benefit are those that are specifically listed in a particular section of the Internal Revenue Code. Distributions from Roth IRAs are not on that list. In fact, many other types of tax-exempt income are not on that list, so there's no reason to think this is an oversight that will be corrected later. In theory it's possible Congress will change this rule, but I don't think that's likely.

Rollovers

You have to report income when you roll a traditional IRA to a Roth IRA, and that income can affect the amount of tax you pay on your social security benefit for the year or years you report the income. If it has this effect, you have to consider this cost when you weigh the your rollover choices.

There's a flip side to this coin. If you don't roll to a Roth IRA, you'll report income when you take distributions from your traditional IRA. That income may increase the portion of your social security benefit that's taxable. As explained above, distributions from a Roth IRA do not affect the tax on your social security benefit. So there's a potential added benefit to a Roth IRA rollover, because it may protect some of your future social security benefits from taxation.

Perspective

These consequences are usually relatively small. They affect you only if your income is within a limited range, because once your income is greater than a certain amount you reach the maximum amount of social security benefit that you have to report. If you're in or close to retirement, it's worth noting these points as you make your decisions about the Roth IRA. But don't be overly influenced by what may turn out to be a negligible effect.

Part VIII
Roth IRA Strategies

A look at some strategies for the Roth IRA.

There are various ways to use a Roth IRA. Here are some ideas, along with discussion about when they work well and when to avoid them.

Part VIII: Roth IRA Strategies

Chapter 46
College Savings

Using the Roth IRA to save for college.

The Roth IRA may not be the best choice if your only savings goal is to pay college expenses. But the Roth IRA can be a key part of a plan to save for college if you're also saving for other purposes such as retirement or the purchase of a home. We'll begin by explaining the basic rules, then see how the Roth IRA can fit into your college savings plans.

College Expenses and IRAs

When you take money from a traditional IRA, you have to pay tax on that amount, no matter how long the money has been in the IRA or how old you are. But if you take a distribution before age 59½, you need to know whether the 10% early distribution penalty tax applies. There are various exceptions to the application of this penalty. One is for qualified higher education expenses, a term that includes most basic college expenses. If the amount you withdraw from your traditional IRA in a given year doesn't exceed the amount of your qualified higher education expenses for that year, the 10% penalty tax won't apply. You'll still have to pay the regular income tax, though.

> **Example:** You withdraw $8,000 to pay college tuition for your child. If you meet the require-

ments to have qualified higher education expenses you won't pay the 10% early distribution penalty tax, but you still have to report the $8,000 as income.

What about the Roth IRA? The special rule for qualified higher education expenses applies to the Roth IRA: it gets you out of paying the early distribution penalty, but it doesn't get you out of paying tax on the amount that would otherwise be taxable.

Example: You have a Roth IRA with a balance of $8,000, consisting of $6,000 in contributions and $2,000 of earnings. You can withdraw up to $6,000 free of tax or penalty, at any time, for any reason. If you withdraw the remaining $2,000 before age 59½, you'll normally pay tax and the 10% early distribution penalty. If you have qualified higher education expenses in the same year you took the distribution, you can withdraw the $2,000 in earnings without paying a penalty, but you still have to pay tax on this income.

Some situations provide you with an exception to both the regular tax and the 10% penalty tax. For example, if you've had a Roth IRA for at least five years and you qualify as a first-time homebuyer, you can withdraw up to $10,000 of earnings without paying tax or penalty. The rule for college expenses only eliminates the penalty.

What this means, as explained in more detail below, is that the Roth IRA may not be the best choice if you plan to apply *all* of your savings to the payment of college expenses. But the Roth IRA may work very well if you plan to use only part of your savings for college expenses, and retain part of your savings for retirement.

College as Single Goal

The Roth IRA provides the greatest benefit when you can take advantage of its most extraordinary feature: the ability to withdraw earnings entirely free of tax. You may get some benefit from a Roth IRA even if you pay tax when you withdraw earnings, but the benefit will be much smaller. And this is precisely the problem with using a Roth IRA for college savings: you may have to pay tax when you withdraw the earnings.

There's no penalty if you take a distribution from an IRA (regular or Roth) for qualified higher education expenses. As explained above, however, you'll still have to pay tax on any earnings you withdraw from a Roth IRA before age 59½ for college expenses.

> **Example:** You're 35, your child is 10. Beginning this year you put $3,000 per year in a Roth IRA. When your child goes to college eight years from now the IRA is worth $40,000 ($24,000 of contributions and $16,000 of earnings).

In the above example you can withdraw your contributions ($24,000) tax free for any purpose you choose. But if you take the $16,000 earnings before you reach age 59½ you must pay tax on those earnings. The only exceptions are for payments to your beneficiary after your death, payments attributable to your being disabled, and the first-time homebuyer exception.

This rule isn't a problem if you'll be over 59½ when you withdraw money from your Roth IRA, because by then all your distributions are tax-free, assuming you've had a Roth for at least five years. But if the earnings will be taxable when you withdraw them, you're missing out on the biggest benefit of the Roth IRA. You still get the benefit of tax-free compounding while your money is in the Roth IRA, but this isn't enough to make the Roth IRA a good choice for college savings if you expect to withdraw earnings while they are taxable.

- We now have other ways to make college savings tax-free. *Coverdell education savings accounts* are similar to Roth IRAs, although they may receive less favorable treatment for financial aid purposes, and they provide less control over the final disposition of the money. State-sponsored college savings programs called *529 accounts* can also produce tax-free earnings if used for qualified purposes.

Roth IRA for Combined Savings

Many people face the challenge of saving for college and saving for retirement at the same time. If you're in this situation, the Roth IRA may permit you to adopt a favorable strategy.

For example, you might feel that you can save only $1,500 per year for retirement during the period you're also saving for college. One approach would be to put $1,500 per year in an IRA and keep the college savings in a separate account (perhaps a Coverdell account or a 529 account).

But there's another choice. You can use the Roth IRA for $1,500 per year of retirement savings and another $1,500 per year of college savings. (Any additional college savings would go into some other account, such as a Coverdell.) You'll consider one-fourth of this account to be part of your college savings. When the time comes to pay for college, you withdraw half of this account. In your mind, you're withdrawing half the contributions and half the earnings, but from the perspective of the IRS you're not withdrawing any earnings until you take out an amount that's larger than your total contributions. And that means your distribution is entirely tax free, unless your earnings have grown so fast that they equal more than half of your account.

What have you accomplished? During the period the college savings were in the Roth IRA, they were accumulating earnings that will never be taxed. If you're saving for college over a long period of time the benefit can be substantial. Meanwhile you've avoided some of the potential drawbacks of Coverdell accounts and 529 accounts. When saving for college and for retirement at the same time, it makes sense to consider whether you can benefit from this strategy.

Chapter 47
Post-Retirement Roth Conversion

It can make sense to convert a traditional IRA to a Roth IRA even after retirement.

Many people believe it doesn't make sense to convert a traditional IRA to a Roth IRA late in life. In reality, a partial or complete conversion can provide significant tax savings even if the owner of the IRA has only a very short life expectancy. The benefits aren't present in all cases, though. Careful analysis is required to determine whether a rollover makes sense, how much to roll over, and when. As explained below, in most cases the rollover will make sense if all of the following are true:

- You'll take only qualified distributions from your Roth IRA, so that all your withdrawals are free from taxes and penalties.

- You'll be able to pay taxes on the rollover from another source. In other words, you won't use money from the IRA to pay taxes.

- Most importantly, you won't pay tax on the rollover at a significantly higher rate than the rate that would apply if you left the money in your traditional IRA, taking it out when you need it later in life. To avoid this problem you may need to do only a partial rollover.

Potential Benefits

A post-retirement rollover may permit you to accomplish one or more of the following:

- Have a larger dollar amount invested in a tax-free vehicle by using other savings to pay tax on the rollover.
- Keep your money invested in a tax-free vehicle for a longer time by avoiding required distributions after age 70½.
- Cause the money in your traditional IRA to be taxed at a lower rate than if your children inherited the IRA.
- Reduce your estate tax by paying income tax on your IRA before you die.

We'll take a closer look at these benefits, then turn to some important points concerning possible detriment.

Increasing the Size of Your IRA

Moving money from a traditional IRA to a Roth IRA has a hidden, but very favorable consequence: it increases the amount of money you have in your IRA. The dollar amount is the same, but the effective amount is larger. This is because the Roth IRA contains only after-tax dollars. Part of your traditional IRA will end up going to Uncle Sam when you cash out, so it's almost as if you don't own the entire IRA. The better your investments do in a traditional IRA, the more taxes end up going to the IRS. That's not true for a Roth IRA. The IRS doesn't share in your investment success, so you truly own the entire account.

Avoiding Required Distributions

Having more money than you need in retirement is a nice problem to have. But that doesn't mean it isn't a problem, if you reach age 70½ and still don't want to take money out of your IRA. If the tax rules force you to take a distribution you don't need, you're losing the benefit of tax-free compounding when you could otherwise be living on other savings. The Roth IRA provides a way to extend the benefits of IRA investing for as long as you can afford to leave the money in the account, and that can mean more wealth for your later years—or for your heirs.

Reducing the Tax Rate on Distributions

If you have reason to believe there will be a substantial amount left in your IRA when you die, you may wish to consider the tax rate that will apply to the benefits. Unless the IRA will be consumed by your spouse, it may pass to children or other heirs while they're in their prime earning years, and therefore in a higher tax bracket than you are. Rolling to a Roth IRA now may avoid having that income taxed at the higher rates that apply to your beneficiaries.

Estate Tax Savings

Most people don't have to worry about federal estate tax because of a credit that effectively exempts $1,500,000 from the tax. (This amount is scheduled to increase over the next several years. See Chapter 30.) If you've accumulated enough wealth to be concerned with the estate tax, a rollover to a Roth IRA may provide an added advantage. The income tax you pay on the rollover reduces the size of your taxable estate (which may reduce the estate tax) without reducing the value of what you leave to your heirs. Estate tax rates are high, so this benefit can be very valuable in those cases where it applies.

Check Your Tax Bracket

Before you roll to a Roth IRA, consider how your tax bracket will affect the overall benefit of the rollover. A high tax bracket can mean the rollover will produce costs that outweigh the benefits.

Even when you're in a favorable tax bracket, you have to watch the size of your rollover. If you roll over too large an amount, the bunching of income into one year can cause you to pay tax at a higher rate than if you withdrew money from your traditional IRA more gradually. With careful planning you may be able to avoid this consequence by controlling the amount you roll over.

> **Example:** You're single and living on social security and pension income. After claiming the standard deduction and personal exemption your taxable income is $10,000, putting you in the 15% bracket. You would like to roll a $100,000 traditional IRA to a Roth IRA. But if you do this, part of the rollover will be taxed at the 25% rate. Your better choice may be to convert an amount that will leave you in the 15% bracket, and do additional conversions in later years.

Tax brackets can catch you in a different way. Suppose you have a traditional IRA and you expect to be able to leave a substantial part of it to your children when you die. If your children are in lower tax brackets, the amount of tax they would pay on receiving the traditional IRA may be less than the amount you would pay on a conversion.

For these reasons, it pays to check carefully to determine what tax bracket you'll be hitting when you make the rollover. You may find that it's best to convert only part of your traditional IRA to a Roth IRA—and in some cases the correct amount to convert is zero.

Determining the right amount to convert isn't terribly difficult if your income is predictable. Some help with this can be found in our web site at www.fairmark.com, particularly on a page in our *Getting Started* guide—look for a page called *Your Tax Bracket*. The current brackets themselves are in the web site's *Reference Room*.

Chapter 48
Roth IRAs for Minors

Can you set up a Roth IRA for a minor child? Should you?

Traditional IRAs haven't been attractive investment vehicles for minors, in part because young children seldom have enough income to benefit from the deduction. A Roth IRA for a child can be very attractive, however. There's no minimum age to set up a Roth IRA, and many IRA providers will accept accounts for minors. In most cases the only issue is whether the child has taxable compensation income. This issue is discussed below.

- Some IRA providers balk at the idea of IRAs for minors, but many mutual funds, brokers and banks accept them, so if you strike out the first time you ask, try again elsewhere.

A Beautiful Idea

Tax-free compounding of earnings inside an IRA is a beautiful idea—and a powerful one. The longer you can keep your money invested in a tax-free vehicle, the greater your wealth accumulation. What better way to accumulate a large amount of savings than to start during childhood? When tax-free compounding has more than

50 years to run its course, a relatively modest savings plan can produce substantial wealth.

There's no minimum (or maximum) age to set up a Roth IRA. And there's no requirement that the same dollars that were earned be used to fund the IRA. If your child earned money on a summer job and spent it on whatever kids spend money on these days,* there's nothing wrong with using money provided by parents to establish the IRA.

A Drawback

Money in your child's IRA belongs to the child. There's no way to restrict the child from withdrawing it and using it in any way he or she chooses, at least after the child reaches the age of majority. Bear this in mind before you pour many thousands of dollars into an IRA for your child.

The Earned Income Requirement

The major impediment to IRAs for children, especially young children, is the earned income requirement. An unmarried person must have earned income of his or her own to contribute to a Roth IRA. The income has to be compensation income, not investment income. And it has to be taxable compensation income. For example, income covered by the foreign earned income exclusion doesn't qualify.

That doesn't mean your child has to actually pay tax on the income. If the total amount of income is small enough so your child doesn't have to pay tax, that's OK. But your child has to have the kind of income that would call for a tax payment if the amount were large enough.

* A recent report says the number one category isn't CDs or video games: it's food.

Example: Your child earns $2,350 bagging groceries after school and during the summer. No tax is due on this amount—the only reason to file an income tax return is to get a refund of any withholding. But your child can contribute to an IRA because the earnings are taxable compensation income.

Income from a Parent's Business

What if the parent is the employer? The fact that the income comes from a parent doesn't disqualify it, although the IRS may take a closer look in cases like this.

There have been a number of cases dealing with parents who paid children to work in the parent's business. None of them deal with the Roth IRA, though. These cases generally deal with the parent's deduction for the amount paid to the child. The Tax Court has recognized the deduction when it was convinced that the parents paid fair compensation for work actually performed in a real business. When the compensation was bogus or didn't relate to a business, the deduction wasn't allowed. Bogus compensation won't support a contribution to a Roth IRA, either.

Household Chores

Why not use a child's earnings from household chores to meet the earned income requirement? Let's make some favorable assumptions:

- The child is actually doing work for the money.
- You're paying only a reasonable hourly rate for the work.
- You have good records to prove that the work was done and the money paid.

Will that do the trick? Strangely enough, there's no clear guidance on this issue. I personally don't believe this form of income can support a contribution to an IRA, because I don't think this income is taxable. So far, though, the IRS hasn't said anything about it, and it isn't clear at this point whether they will raise the issue.

It's rather bold on my part to suggest that this form of income isn't taxable, because the Internal Revenue Code says all income is taxable unless an exception is made, and there's no exception for amounts paid by parents to minor children for household chores. No explicit exception, anyway. Yet I'm comfortable in the conclusion.

The situation is somewhat like the question that came up about Mark McGuire's 62nd home run ball. Apparently someone at the IRS said that if a fan who caught the ball gave it to McGuire, there would be a gift tax on the transfer. The statement caused an uproar because it was so absurd. There isn't any exception that applies to that situation. According to the law as written, the fan does have a gift tax liability. But everyone understood that the law wasn't intended to apply that way, and the Commissioner of the IRS hastened to say so in a public statement.

It would be equally absurd to say that minor children have to pay tax when parents pay them for household chores. Everyone knows that instinctively. No one reports this income, and the IRS never challenges it. It isn't a case where millions of people are cheating and getting away with it; it's simply a case where it never occurred to anyone in Congress that an exception had to be written into the law. The income simply isn't taxable. But don't take my word for it. Here's what Boris Bittker, a legal scholar who is perhaps the leading authority on this type of issue, has to say on the subject:

> "Intrafamily transfers of this type can be properly viewed as excludable by a higher authority than the language of [the

> Internal Revenue Code]—a supposition, so obvious that it does not require explicit mention in the Code, that Congress never intended to tax them."

If the income isn't taxable, it can't support an IRA contribution. You can't turn it into "good" income for this purpose by choosing to treat it as taxable income. It either is or it isn't. In my view it isn't.

Tax Consequences

As I mentioned earlier, the IRS hasn't shown any interest in this issue—so far. Possibly they never will, and no one will ever have problems with IRAs set up for children.

If the IRS does decide to crack down, however, the consequences can be severe. A contribution that isn't supported by taxable compensation income is an excess contribution. There's a 6% penalty that applies to this contribution if it isn't withdrawn (together with earnings) by the return due date for the year of the contribution. And the penalty applies again for each subsequent year the money is left in the IRA. If the money sits in the IRA for 5 years before the mistake is discovered, the penalty is 30%. After 10 years it's 60%, and so on. The only way to stop the penalty from running is to take the money out of the IRA, including any earnings. And when you remove the earnings they'll be taxable, plus subject to a 10% early distribution penalty. Overall, the worst case is fairly ugly.

Some people will suggest that it's unlikely the IRS will ever go after kiddie IRAs in this way, and they may be right. You may be missing a golden opportunity if you fail to set one up. In the case of a minor child whose only "income" is from doing household chores for parents, you should be aware that there's some reason to doubt whether the contribution is proper, and at least some risk of incurring penalties.

Chapter 49
Wash Sales and IRAs

If you sell stock at a loss, is it OK to buy it again right away in your IRA?

The concern, of course, is the wash sale rule. If you buy the same stock right away in a regular brokerage account, the wash sale rule says you can't deduct the loss on your sale. It's natural to wonder if you can avoid this rule by buying the stock in an IRA. If it worked, this approach would allow you to have your cake and eat it too: you would get to deduct your loss while continuing your investment in that particular stock without interruption.

- Visit the guide to capital gains on our web site at www.fairmark.com for full details on the wash sale rule.

There's plenty of confusion about this rule, even among tax professionals. The answer, according to the IRS, is that you lose the deduction if you buy replacement shares in your IRA. The problem is that the answer isn't easy to find.

Wash Sales and Related Parties

If Congress were writing the wash sale rule today, they would make it apply to related parties. They did that for more recent rules dealing with financial transactions, such as the constructive sale rule. Yet the wash sale rule is relatively ancient and has never been brought up to date. Nothing in the law says it applies to related parties.

If that were the end of the story, you could go ahead and buy replacement stock in an IRA. You could also have your spouse or another relative buy replacement stock, or use an entity you control (such as a corporation, a trust or a family partnership) to buy replacement stock. No one would have to worry about the wash sale rule because it would be so easily avoided. That sounds too good to be true, and it is. But why?

Sales to Related Parties

The wash sale rule is only one of the rules that can prevent you from claiming a deduction when you sell stock at a loss. You lose the deduction also if you sell to a related person. In the special language of the tax law, a "person" includes not only human beings, but also entities like the ones mentioned above: corporations, trusts, partnerships — anything that can be used to maintain indirect ownership of other assets, including stock.

If you sell stock at a loss to a related person, you can't deduct the loss. What's worse, unlike a wash sale, a sale to a related person prevents you or the related person from claiming a loss deduction on a later sale. That's a painful result, but you may be wondering what it has to do with the original question. No one ever said anything about selling stock to an IRA. The idea is to sell the stock to a stranger, then use the IRA to buy replacement shares, presumably from a different stranger.

Indirect Sales

The IRS says a sale and purchase occurring about the same time should be treated as an indirect sale to a related person if they occurred together as part of a plan.

Their position is backed up by decisions where courts ruled in favor of the IRS. Here's a quote from IRS Publication 550:

> **Indirect transactions.** You cannot deduct your loss on the sale of stock through your broker if, under a prearranged plan, a related party buys the same stock you had owned. This does not apply to a trade between related parties through an exchange that is purely coincidental and is not prearranged.

The IRS allows for the possibility that a purchase of replacement shares could occur by coincidence, for example if you and your adult child are both active investors who trade independently. Realistically, no one is going to believe the transactions were coincidental if the same person directed both of them. And that's exactly what's going on when you sell stock in a brokerage account and buy replacement shares in an IRA.

The IRS position is backed up by a ruling by the Supreme Court in a 1947 case called McWilliams (331 US 694). That case deals with a situation where a husband sold stock at a loss and had his broker buy replacement shares for his wife's account. I can't think of a good reason to treat repurchase in an IRA any differently.

Caveat Lector

It's possible you'll find a contrary opinion, perhaps even from a reputable tax professional. The main reason for this is that you can study the wash sale rule all you want without finding anything about related parties. Most people won't even think of the rule for sales to related parties, because you aren't actually selling to your IRA.

Another reason for confusion is that the tax law uses rather arcane language to tell us when a trust is a "related person." It's easy to get hung up in that language and convince yourself that an IRA isn't related to its owner.

Common sense tells you otherwise, and so does the tax law if you can work through the technicalities.

According to one article I saw, an IRS agent posted an answer to this question on the IRS web site saying it was OK to buy replacement shares in an IRA. Every year the IRS gives many thousands of incorrect answers in informal guidance of this kind. The official position of the IRS is the one quoted earlier from Publication 550, not the offhand response of an agent responding to an email question.

Reality Check

The wash sale rule and the rule for sales to related parties work together for a single purpose: to prevent you from claiming a loss deduction while maintaining uninterrupted ownership of your stock. If you aren't willing to part with the stock, you aren't eligible for the deduction. Buying replacement shares in an IRA is a gimmick designed to defeat the basic purpose of these provisions. It shouldn't work, and if the IRS position in Publication 550 is upheld, it won't.

Chapter 50
Liquidating a Roth IRA for a Loss

If your Roth IRA has lost enough value, you may gain a tax benefit from liquidating it.

If you've lost money in your Roth IRA, you're not alone. We had three years of a sour stock market, and despite a recent recovery there's plenty of pain to go around. Some investments have lost value dramatically.

If your Roth loses money shortly after you converted from a traditional IRA, your best choice is probably to undo the conversion. After waiting long enough you can convert again, assuming you still qualify for a conversion. Usually the lower value of the account means you'll pay a smaller tax on the second conversion. But what if it's too late to undo the conversion?

Loss on Liquidation

Ordinarily, distributions from a traditional IRA are taxable, so the tax "benefit" when your account loses value is that you report a reduced amount of income rather than claiming a loss deduction. Yet if you've made nondeductible contributions to a traditional IRA, you recover those contributions—your IRA's "basis"—free of tax. If your account ends up with a value smaller than its basis, the IRS allows a deduction, but only if you completely liquidate all your traditional IRAs.

For technical reasons, it wasn't always clear that this deduction is available for Roth IRAs. Since 2001, though, IRS Publication 590 gives a favorable answer: if you liquidate all your Roth IRAs for an amount that's less than your basis, you can claim a deduction for your loss. Your basis is the amount of your contributions to the Roth, including conversion contributions, reduced by any amounts you've withdrawn.

What Kind of Deduction?

You might expect to get a capital loss deduction in this situation. After all, in most cases the IRA lost value because stocks, mutual funds or other investments in the IRA declined. Instead, the IRS says this is a miscellaneous itemized deduction that's subject to the 2% floor. Here's what that means.

On the good side, this is an "ordinary" deduction rather than a capital loss. That means the $3,000 capital loss limitation doesn't apply, and the deduction counts against income that's taxed at the highest rate that applies to you.

There's a drawback, though. The deduction is available only if you itemize. If you normally claim the standard deduction, it may pay to consider itemizing to claim your IRA loss. But if your loss isn't big enough, you might still be better off with the standard deduction, and that means you get no benefit from liquidating your IRA.

And there's another drawback: the 2% floor. All your deductions that fall into this category of "miscellaneous" itemized deductions get lumped together and reduced by 2% of your adjusted gross income (AGI). If you don't have other miscellaneous deductions, the entire 2% reduction comes out of your IRA deduction.

Example: You converted a traditional IRA when it was worth $5,000 and now it's worth $1,500. Your

> AGI is $90,000. If you liquidate the Roth for a loss of $3,500, you'll have to reduce that amount by $1,800 (2% of your AGI), leaving you with a deduction of only $1,700.

And there's another drawback. Miscellaneous deductions aren't allowed for purposes of the alternative minimum tax (AMT). That means you could lose the benefit of the deduction (or some of the benefit) because of the AMT rules. This type of AMT situation doesn't give rise to an AMT credit you can recover in future years, so any part of the deduction that gets swallowed up in the AMT is lost forever.

Liquidating Your IRA

To qualify for the deduction for losses in a Roth IRA, you have to liquidate all your Roth IRAs. You can't claim a loss on one Roth while keeping another Roth in place, even if all the loss occurred in one Roth. The same rule applies to traditional IRAs where the value is less than your basis. However, you don't have to liquidate traditional IRAs to claim your loss in a Roth, or vice versa.

Bear in mind that if you converted from a traditional IRA, liquidation of your Roth will result in a penalty equal to 10% of the distribution if you're under 59½ and the distribution occurs before the fifth year after the conversion. If your account still has substantial value, you may want to delay liquidation of a conversion Roth IRA even though this will delay your deduction. You don't have to worry about this if your Roth has only annual (non-conversion) contributions because the penalty for that type of Roth applies only to earnings. A Roth isn't considered to have earnings if the value has decreased, even if the Roth received amounts like interest and dividends that would normally be considered earnings.

Is It Worth It?

Whether it makes sense to liquidate your Roth to claim this deduction depends on many factors. Do you itemize? How large is the loss compared with 2% of your AGI? How much do you lose by removing what's left of your account from the Roth IRA, where it has the potential to produce tax-exempt earnings? Will you incur a 10% penalty if you liquidate now? This can be a complicated decision, so you may want to consult with a tax professional before making this move.

Index

Notes

Notes

also from Fairmark Press:

Consider Your Options

Get the Most from Your Equity Compensation

This is the leading book on how to handle all the popular forms of equity compensation: stock grants, nonqualified stock options, incentive stock options and employee stock purchase plans. *Consider Your Options* has been popular with option holders for its clarity, and with tax professionals and financial advisors for its thoroughness and accuracy.

Capital Gains, Minimal Taxes

The Essential Guide for Investors and Traders

This book makes it easy to understand the rules—and the best strategies for minimizing taxes. In plain language it covers tax rules that apply to anyone who buys and sells stocks, mutual funds and market-traded stock options. It starts from the most basic rules but includes advanced material such as straddles and constructive sales. It also covers the tax treatment of people who qualify as traders.

Visit our web site at www.fairmark.com for more information, including online ordering and volume discounts—or use the order form on the reverse.

Order Form

Order more of our books from our web site (**www.fairmark.com**), or by mailing or faxing a copy of this form.

Fax: (630) 434-0753

Mail: Fairmark Press Inc.
P.O. Box 353
Lisle, IL 60532

Quantity		
______	*Fairmark Guide to the Roth IRA* @ $13.95	________
______	*Consider Your Options* @ $23.95	________
______	*Capital Gains, Minimal Taxes* @ $19.95	________
	Total for books	________
	Shipping (flat rate per order)	$4.00
	Total	________

Illinois residents add 6.75% sales tax.

Ship to:

Name: ____________________

Address: ____________________

Address: ____________________

City, State, zip: ____________________

Phone: ____________________

Email: ____________________

Payment

__________ Check ____ VISA ____ MasterCard
________ AMEX ____ Discover

Card number: ____________________

Exp. date: ____________________

Credit Card Info (if different from shipping)

Billing name: ____________________

Address: ____________________

City, State, zip: ____________________